I0092754

THE ENNEAGRAM EXPLAINED:

SUPERCHARGE YOUR SELF-DISCOVERY JOURNEY, UNCOVER YOUR TRUE PERSONALITY & UNDERSTAND ALL 9 ENNEATYPES PLUS UNIQUE TIPS & PRACTICES FOR ALL 9 TYPES

ENNEAGRAM UNWRAPPED

BOOK ONE

PERSONALITY HUB

CONTENTS

THE PURPOSE OF
THIS BOOK

To help people uncover their Type. This book explains each of the nine types in detail and provides fun examples that are easy to relate to.

Accompanying each Type are practical tips on the lifestyle changes you can make and some daily practices that are more effective for your specific Type.

INTRODUCTION

What if I told you that your quest for material success and the current goals you've set will do nothing more but delight you for a short while, after which you'll plunge right back into that endless pit of restlessness plaguing your life?

Look around you. The world appears to be more chaotic than ever. There's so much doom and gloom everywhere. Countries continue to war against each other; discrimination, instability, disruption, and hate seem to be the trend. And those who aren't busy spreading hate are working themselves to death trying to be the next big sensation on the Internet.

What is happening to humanity? Have we lost our way? Are we becoming worse as technological advancements continue? Shouldn't we be more at peace, in love, fulfilled, and at one with each other as globalization becomes the order of the day?

It turns out that human beings are great at many things. We can solve big problems, such as traveling across the planet, getting to the moon, and even more complex things like how to eliminate fossil fuels. But, unfortunately, we're terrible at solving the simple problem of finding peace and fulfillment. And unless each human can begin to feel peaceful, fulfilled, happy, and secure in their own life, we will continue to witness the horrible state of the world. And this doesn't only apply to global issues. Think about your own life, where you work, your health, your relationships, and your current lifestyle. How satisfied, fulfilled, and happy are you with what you see when you look in the mirror?

The fact is, if you had found your fulfillment and peace in life, this book would have no appeal to you. I may not know your unique situation, but allow me to risk the credibility of this book by boldly stating the following.

It doesn't matter what you think you desire in life; the real thing you're seeking is a sense of connection, security, and unconditional love. You're seeking peace and fulfillment. You want the "thing" that will finally make you feel complete and whole. Unfortunately, you'll never find that by chasing after a "thing."

So, I'm glad you're here because I can promise you this: if you stick with this book and commit to applying everything you learn, you will break the chains of bondage and lift the veil of illusion that had you chasing after the wrong desires. This book will empower you to have the freedom to know, be, and love yourself.

And when you know, love, and live from your true Self, you become unstoppable on the playground of life. Does that sound like something you'd be interested in? Good. Then let's get started.

KNOW THYSELF

"Know thyself" sounds like a cliché, and maybe it is, but I stand by it nonetheless. It is the golden secret to a life beyond your dreams.

As far back as ancient Greece, people have been seeking this knowledge of self.

Few can quench an unshakeable thirst to understand who we are, what we want, and what it takes to experience happiness and fulfillment in life. Entire disciplines exist around this topic of understanding more about ourselves as humans. Most of it only amplifies our differences and breeds wild egos that cause more harm than good.

I am not here to offer scientific lectures. Instead, I want to present a simple solution that can enable you to explore and discover the Truth for yourself.

Our behavior directly results from our character and personality, which typically start taking shape during our childhood years. The core beliefs and values that we hold deep in our subconscious minds make us distinct in approaching and reacting to life. One individual's likes, dislikes, fears, strengths, and weaknesses will lead to different responses compared to another's, even if the two people are facing the same obstacle. What creates this difference? How we grow up, the perspectives and worldviews we hold, and our beliefs, whether true or false, affect our actions, health, life-style, and well-being. They make us what we are.

Can you imagine a world in which, instead of using gender, skin color, culture, etc., to determine our identity, we focused on understanding our personality type? What kind of a world would that be?

Don't get me wrong, I'm not saying culture and beliefs are bad. But I can confidently say that there would be better relationships, more compassion, and communities that function efficiently in such a world. This book isn't here to point fingers or establish black and white rules over what's good and what's bad. Life isn't binary. As you get to know your true Self, the discovery you'll make is that the spectrum of life is vast enough to accommodate all differences. The self-discovery quest is transformational and priceless because it finally enables you to understand unity and wholeness. And when one attains that knowledge, nothing in their world is ever the same.

Why did you desire to read this book?

Are you among those who feel broken in some way? Is there an inner restlessness or void that you're trying to resolve? Or perhaps you've realized that success can only come from within, and now you're trying to figure out what "within" means.

I find it good practice to always ask myself, "Why am I doing this thing?" Whenever I clarify my reason for doing something, I always seem to get the most out of that activity.

Regardless of your reasons, I'm glad you're here. This is the right time and season in your life to embark on a journey of self-discovery, to get answers about who you are, why you're here, and what life is all about.

Material success, romantic relationships, and career opportunities can flow more naturally into your life as you get to know yourself more. But don't limit yourself to "getting things ."If love is what you're after, don't limit it to finding a soul mate. Even if you manifest that ideal lover, it will not satiate and fill that void that caused you to yearn for love. If abundance is what you seek, don't limit it to making more money because no amount of money will ever satisfy the feeling of lack and insecurity you have. What you need is abundance and a real sense of security, neither of which can be permanently found in acquiring more money. So before we jump into the specifics of this book, let's clarify what this book can do for you and whom it's intended for.

WHAT THIS BOOK IS AND HOW TO USE IT

This book aims to enable you, dear reader, to finally discover who you really are. It's not about superficially identifying common traits or giving gimmicks that will allow you to manifest whatever you seek. Instead, this is about unlocking your potential. Regardless of your past experiences, upbringing, and environment, who you are is mostly untapped potential. To the extent that you've lost touch with your true self, you will experience the restlessness that most humans try to cover up with material possessions and mindless activities.

The rewards of going through this book:

In this book, you'll find practical tips and specific transformational processes tailored to your Enneagram type. You'll also learn how to cultivate present moment awareness, become better at catching old negative thoughts and behaviors, and gently dissolve those limiting behaviors. Last but not least, you'll get tips on the lifestyle changes you can make and some daily practices that are more effective for your specific Type. Before you begin this quest, I encourage you to get a private journal, notebook, or digital diary where you can take personal notes as you discover new exercises. This is also where you'll record the insights that come to you as you learn about your personality type and the other eight types. Throughout the ensuing chapters, you'll find simple yet powerful exercises that I suggest you consistently engage in. Don't shortchange yourself. Remember, the whole purpose of the Enneagram is to discover your true self. Unless you're willing to be honest and clear about your needs and wants and committed to doing the inner work, this tool will not yield much. What you put in is what you'll get out of the Enneagram tool. Okay, time to clear up the mystery behind the Enneagram tool, what it is, and how it works.

SECTION 1

INTRODUCTION TO THE ENNEAGRAM

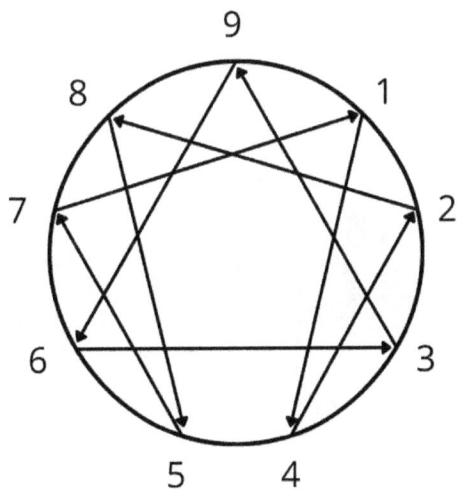

CHAPTER I

THE ENNEAGRAM SYSTEM

T he Enneagram (*pronounced ANY-a-gram*) is a personality typing system that uses a nine-pointed geometrical diagram to illustrate nine core personality types in the human race and how each Type relates to the other. The term *Ennea* is Greek for "nine," and *Grammos* means "figure." Thus, it is a nine-pointed figure.

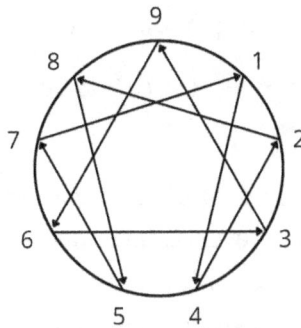

According to the Enneagram system, each of these nine personality types is defined by a particular core belief and frame of mind about how the world works. That core belief drives the Type's deepest fears and highest motivations. When we discover our true Type, we can see how our core beliefs shape our worldview and the lens through which we see others, ourselves, and the world. The Enneagram system aims to teach us that, for the most part, we are working with limited core beliefs. The beliefs may not be harmful per se, just excessively limiting, and may thus become "blinders" that block our minds. Using the Enneagram tool aims to increase our awareness of how our core beliefs color our perceptions so we can ultimately broaden our perspective and approach life more effectively. We look to the Enneagram system to help us discover and understand ourselves better (why do we behave as we do when we're sad, stressed, happy, etc.). And in knowing more about ourselves, we can start to understand why others react and behave as they do. To call it a personality typing system doesn't nearly do it justice. The Enneagram has a long history, and it has evolved over time to become the modern tool that we've adopted here in the West. But we should always remember that, at a fundamental level, the Enneagram's purpose is to awaken and elevate you to greater spiritual heights, not just give you information about personality traits.

Here's an excellent way to think about the Enneagram system:

Imagine yourself running into the ocean for an early morning swim. As the sun rises, everything on the surface is calm; the water is cool, and the sensation of the salty water on your skin feels invigorating. You're swimming on the ocean's surface, and it's impossible to see the world that exists far beneath you from that vantage point. To access that world, you need special gear and a trained professional. But just because you don't see what lies beneath the surface doesn't mean it doesn't exist. You can enjoy the ocean water at the surface with fellow humans, but if you really want to know and experience the true wonders of the ocean, you'll need to swim deep and go where most humans aren't willing to go. If you have the right gear and a good guide, that experience will be transformational. You will never look at the ocean the same way again.

While this is a trivial illustration, it can enable you to gain the proper perspective when it comes to understanding the Enneagram's purpose. Some people only want to stay on the surface, and that's okay. For such people, the Enneagram will tell them their ennea type and what traits correspond to their Type. But the Enneagram tool can also be used to uncover a world you never knew existed. That's what I hope you're here to explore and experience. But I'm getting ahead of myself. Let's first trace the origins and history of this tool before introducing the enneatype.

A BRIEF HISTORY OF THE ENNEAGRAM TOOL

To understand the history of the modern Enneagram tool, we need to clarify a common misunderstanding. The Enneagram symbol and the nine personality types have different origins. The Enneagram symbol is ancient, dating back 2,500 years or more. Indeed, the exact origins of the symbol have been lost to history. The roots of the nine personality types also date far back, perhaps as early as the 4th century A.D. in Alexandria, where a Christian mystic called Evagrius Ponticus identified the eight "deadly thoughts" (or *logismoi*) and an overarching thought that translates to "self-love." Ponticus devoted his life to exploring these thoughts and worked to find a solution to counteract the eight deadly ones. At the time, no one used the term Enneagram, but as you continue to study the tool, you'll make a connection between this modern-day system and the works of Ponticus.

Fast forward to the 19th century, we encounter the man credited with bringing the Enneagram symbol to the modern world. His name was George Ivanovich Gurdjieff. Gurdjieff was a Greek-Armenian born around 1875, and as a young man, he became fascinated with esoteric knowledge. Gurdjieff believed in the existence of a complete science for transforming the human psyche and devoted his entire life to searching for these lost teachings that would enable human beings to find their place in the universe and their purpose.

Through his extensive study and the knowledge he and his colleagues gathered, a synthesized teaching was born that integrated spirituality, psychology, and cosmology. Gurdjieff taught that the Enneagram (which he'd discovered during his travels) was the central and most important symbol in his philosophy. Although Gurdjieff taught using the Enneagram symbol, it wasn't yet a model for psychology, but rather a model of natural processes. Gurdjieff explained that the Enneagram symbol has three parts representing the Divine Laws governing all existence. The first is the circle, which represents unity, wholeness, oneness, and the idea that God is One. The second is the triangle drawn within the circle. The triangle represents trinity, or what Gurdjieff called the Law of Threes, which states everything that exists results from the interaction of three forces (whatever they may be in a given situation or dimension). You'll notice many triads in the Enneagram teachings throughout this book.

The third and last part of the Enneagram symbol is the hexad (the figure that traces the points 1-4-2-8-5-7 in our modern Enneagram symbol. Gurdjieff called this the "Law of Seven," which has to do with process and development over time. He taught that everything constantly changes and moves according to its own nature and the forces acting on them. We get the Enneagram symbol by combining these three parts, i.e., the circle, triangle, and hexad. Gurdjieff taught this philosophy through sacred dances explaining that it should be thought of as a living symbol that was dynamic and ever in motion. It should, however, be noted that Gurdjieff did not teach the Enneagram tool as a personality tool. The combination of the Enneagram symbol and the personality types took place only a few decades ago in the 20th century.

The modern version of the Enneagram symbol and the nine points has been developed according to the teachings of Oscar Ichazo, a Bolivian teacher, healer, and philosopher. Ichazo was just as passionate as Gurdjieff about uncovering lost knowledge. Through extensive study, research, and travel, he synthesized the many elements of the Enneagram symbol and found the connection between the symbol and the personality types.

Ichazo's teachings describe concepts like virtue, holy ideas, passion, and ego. All these are considered traits that represent the basis of the nine personalities of the Enneagram. Ichazo is also credited for coining the term "Enneagram of personality." His young budding student, Claudio Naranjo, developed this method of determining personality into the different branches we see today. Naranjo, a Chilean psychiatrist, had a different view of the Enneagram and wanted to expand it in new ways. That led to other influencers like Jesuit priests also taking the initiative to combine Christian spirituality and the Enneagram of self-discovery and regulation. Others like Don Richard Riso, Helem Palmer, Richard Rohr, and Eli Jaxon Bear were influenced by the works of Naranjo and continue to share their own versions of the Enneagram tool.

For our own point of reference, we can deduce that the Enneagram symbol we know and love here in the West is a synthesis of many different spiritual and religious traditions. Much of what we know about it is a condensation of universal wisdom and philosophies accumulated by Christians, Buddhists, Muslims, and Jews for thousands of years. Though it was passed on from teacher to teacher over the centuries, one thing remains untainted. That is the agreement across all branches of the Enneagram system that we are more than just flesh and bones. We are, in fact, spiritual beings having human experiences. Beneath the surface, regardless of all the differences we seem to have, over and above the veils of illusion, we are pure light and love. Unfortunately, we have given power to obstacles and forces that obscure the light we are and therefore have created a disconnect that each of us experiences as a form of restlessness and void. The Sufi Poet Rumi was accurate and overly wise when he said, "Your task is not to seek our love, but merely to seek and find all the barriers within yourself that you have built against it." This is a call of freedom, your freedom. And the Enneagram system will map out the quest you must embark on to finally attain this absolute freedom. Are you ready?

In the ensuing chapters, you will learn how to interpret the Enneagram symbol and all the nine points so you can apply the teachings to suit the current modern environment we live in.

WHAT YOU NEED TO KNOW ABOUT THE ENNEAGRAM AND HOW IT WORKS

The Enneagram work begins when you learn to identify your Type. This personality typing system describes how you may interpret feelings toward yourself and others. It is a complex framework that consists of nine different personality types, three subtypes, three centers of intelligence, and eighteen distinct wings. Don't be overwhelmed by the complexity of this symbol when you see all the different aspects. Think of these as layers that enable you to go deeper into your quest of self-discovery. As I said before, you are at liberty to decide whether you'll stay at the surface level and use it to determine your personality only or dive deeper to discover who you really are. What makes the Enneagram unique and different from other personality typing systems, e.g., the Myers–Briggs personality typing system, is that you won't just be placed into a rigid category. Instead, you'll see your personality spectrum and the growth opportunities you have to unlock your fullest potential. In other words, the Enneagram affords you the gift of true self-discovery and increased personal awareness.

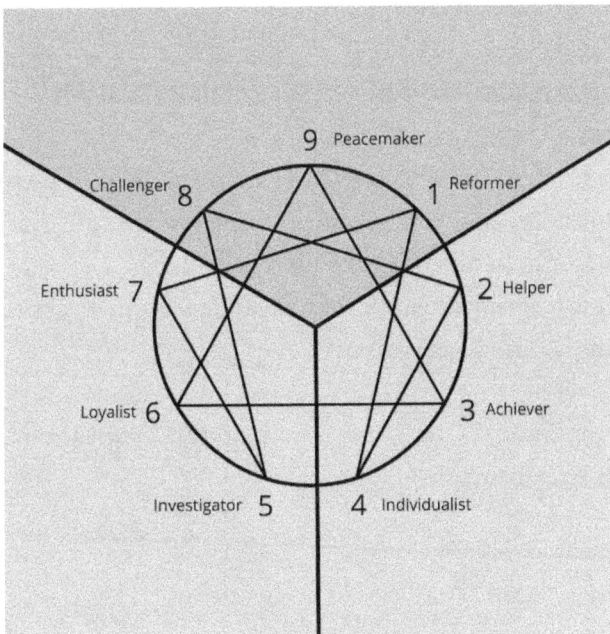

To understand what that diagram means, take note of the outer circle on which the nine personalities are marked. The numbers are evenly spaced around this circle because the circle represents wholeness and the unity and oneness of life. Inside the circle, a triangle connects the numbers 3, 6, and 9. Notice also the hexagonal shape connecting the other numbers, with each Type being joined by two lines to two other personalities. There's another layer to become aware of here. Notice the numbers on each side of any particular type (e.g., Type 3 will have adjacent to it 2 and 4). These adjacent personality types become Wings for that particular Enneatype. They represent the personalities that can influence that Type in different circumstances. We'll unpack all these different layers as the book unfolds, but for now, I invite you to sit in quiet observation for a moment or two before moving to the next chapter. See if you can find some resonance with the symbol above.

Ask yourself questions like:

- Do I feel resonance with the idea of unity and wholeness of life?
- Does it make sense to me that I am not just a single rigid personality, and that specific influences can shift my behavior depending on the circumstance?
- Does it feel right to approach myself as a spiritual being having a human experience?

If you answered yes to all or most of these questions, let the inward journey begin.

CHAPTER 2

THE FIRST STEP IS TAKING A JOURNEY INWARD

The quest for self-discovery is an inward journey that begins the moment one makes a solid commitment that they will stop living from the inside out. Until you decide to stop approaching life as others have, you will not get the most out of this book or the Enneagram tool. I believe you're here because you want transformation. If so, make the decision that, from this moment on, you will no longer play as a victim in life and instead approach it as a co-creative experience. The fact is, you are co-creating the story of your life, and the more connected you are to your higher self, the less random life becomes. The Enneagram tool facilitates this shift from living outside-in to living inside-out. The first step is to identify your Enneagram Type.

INTRODUCING THE NINE TYPES

The Enneagram tool will begin to serve its purpose in your life as you identify your Type and understand your Type's most dominant issues. If you recognize a bit of yourself in more than one

Type, that's perfectly normal. There's a little bit of us in every Type because we are all connected, but our most defining characteristics are rooted in one of the nine Types. That's what you want to hone in. At the end of this chapter, you'll find a questionnaire developed by Riso and Hudson called the Riso-Hudson Quest that will help you narrow down your primary Type. Then as you go through each of the Enneagram Type chapters, you'll have the chance to dig deeper and learn a little more about each Type. By the time you're done reading all the descriptions and doing the exercises provided, you should have a firm grasp of your personality type. However, if you want to be extra certain, you can go online and take a final Enneagram test to see how you score and whether your self-assessment matches the professional assessment. Some tests are free, but the best ones tend to be paid. I will leave some links in the resource section of this book for both free and paid online tests.

For now, read the brief descriptions for each Type to see if you can spot two or three that strike you as most typical of yourself. Creating a shortlist of two or three as you go through this book is an excellent first step toward narrowing down this process. That way, you can give these as much attention as possible when going through self-discovery exercises. Keep in mind the characteristics listed in this chapter are merely an introduction and do not represent the full spectrum of each personality.

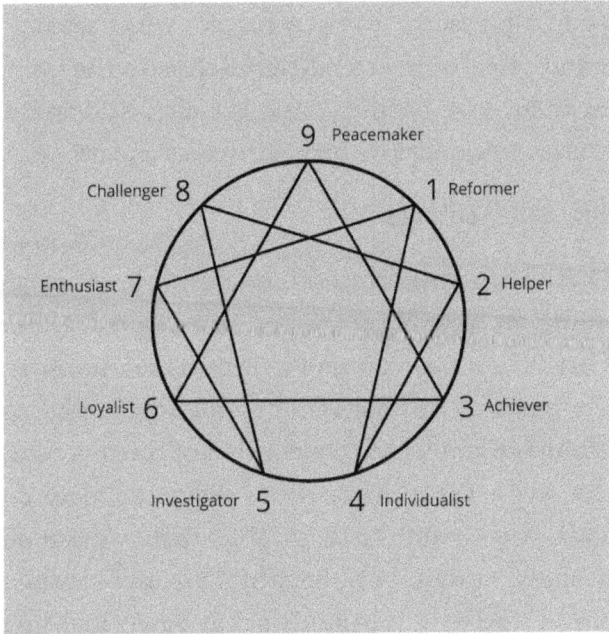

The enneagram diagram showing the nine types arranged around a circle: 9 Peacemaker (top), 1 Reformer, 2 Helper, 3 Achiever, 4 Individualist, 5 Investigator, 6 Loyalist, 7 Enthusiast, 8 Challenger.

Type One: The Reformer

They are the highly moral, principled, and idealistic Type. Ones are ethical and conscientious, with a strong sense of right and wrong. They tend to be the teachers, crusaders, and activists who strive to improve things and are super afraid of error. Ones are organized, orderly, and fastidious. They have extremely high standards, which can lead to perfectionism. Ones have problems with repressed anger and impatience. At their best, healthy Ones are wise, noble, realistic, discerning, and morally heroic.

Type Two: The Helper

They are the caring, nurturing Type. Twos are empathetic, warm-hearted, sincere, friendly, and generous. Think of that self-sacrificing person who is always putting themselves first and is naturally great at developing solid relationships. Twos are driven to be close to others and often do things for others to be needed. As serious people-pleasers, Twos struggle with setting healthy bounders and often over-extend themselves to the point of self-neglect. At their best, healthy Twos are altruistic and unselfish. They ooze unconditional love for themselves and others.

Type Three: The Achiever

Threes are the adaptable, success-oriented Type. They are attractive, charming, ambitious, competent, self-assured, and energetic, and most are very status conscious. Threes are usually concerned about their personal advancement, some even more concerned about their image and what others think of them. A fundamental struggle for Type Threes is knowing when to slow down and relax. That's why many have trouble with workaholism and competitiveness. At their best, healthy Threes are authentic, self-accepting, and tend to be role models that others look up to.

Type Four: The Individualist

They are the introspective, romantic Type. Fours are highly sensitive, emotionally attuned to themselves and others, self-aware, and reserved. Some can come across as highly moody depending on their level of development, but, in all cases, they tend to be emotionally honest and self-revealing. Fours typically have trouble with the victim mindset and often engage in self-pity. At their best, healthy Fours are highly creative, inspired, and able to renew themselves and transform experiences from mundane to magical.

Type Five: The Investigator

They are the intense, logical, cerebral Type, with an insatiable curiosity and a thirst for knowledge. Thinking is a Type Five's comfort zone. Fives are typically highly alert, insightful, and focused. They can concentrate on things for a long time and tackle extremely complex ideas that the rest of us wouldn't dare. And the best part is they do it with such grace and poise that we can't help but admire them. Perhaps you've encountered such a person, or you are that person.

Fives are independent and innovative, but they can easily become too detached from the world and relationships with others. They typically have problems with eccentricity, isolation, and nihilism. At their best, healthy Fives are visionary pioneers and often ahead of their time. They see the world in an entirely new way.

Type Six: The Loyalist

Loyalists are committed, reliable, hardworking, responsible, and security-oriented. They are often cautious and indecisive, though some can also be rebellious, defiant, and reactive, especially under high stress. Sixes have trouble trusting others and themselves, so they often grapple with suspicion and self-doubt. At their best, healthy Sixes are confident, emotionally stable, courageous, self-reliant, and most enjoy championing the weak and powerless.

Type Seven: The Enthusiast

They are the busy, productive Type, always playful and high-spirited. Sevens are optimistic, spontaneous, versatile, and crave adventure. Seeking out new and exciting experiences that amplify pleasure is a Seven's comfort zone. Although Sevens tend to be multitalented and passionate about their various activities, they can easily overextend themselves and become scattered and undisciplined. Sevens typically struggle with impulsiveness and a fear of commitment. At their best, healthy Sevens are joyous, focused, purposeful, highly accomplished, and full of gratitude. They know how to see things through to completion without losing their sense of freedom and adventure.

Type Eight: The Challenger

Eights are powerful, dominating, confident, strong, assertive, and resourceful. They believe that they must be in control of their environment at all times and aren't afraid to be confrontational and intimidating if that's what it takes to win respect. They can also be prideful and domineering. Many Eights have to grapple with vulnerability and let in those they love because, for the most part, they associate intimacy and emotions with weakness. At their best, healthy Eights are heroic, magnanimous, and strong. They have the strong urge and potential to become historically significant in society.

Type Nine: The Peacemaker

Nines are easy-going, calm, trusting, accepting, and stable. They are kind-hearted, gentle, good-natured, and very supportive, and people just love being around them. Some Nines can easily go too far and lose their identity in the name of "fitting in" and keeping the peace. Their strong desire for stability and peace often causes them to avoid confrontation at all costs. They typically struggle with passive-aggressiveness, loss of identity, and hidden anger issues. At their best, healthy Nines have the powerful gift of bringing healing and understanding wherever they are. They can bring people together, heal conflicts, and create a sense of stability that allows others to let their guard down.

Now that you've had a brief introduction to the Nine Enneagram Types, you may have been drawn to certain qualities that felt very real for you. If not, that's pretty normal too. Various indicators will enable you to determine your primary personality type. These include the Wings, Sub-types, and Centers of Intelligence. Let's elaborate on what each of these is.

WHAT ARE WINGS?

Enneagram Wings are the numbers located on each side of your Enneagram Type. So if you discover you're a Type Two, your Wings would naturally be One and Three; if you're a Type Six, then your Wings are Five and Seven. Why are Wings important? Our Wings enable us to "borrow" and become influenced by the energy and qualities of said Wings. Having Wings adds a lot of depth to our overall Enneagram Type. The borrowing of energy shows in real action as similar traits and qualities. The jury is still out whether we're influenced by both Wings equally or whether we only rely on a single Wing. Some teachers emphasize the two-Wing theory, which makes sense because it offers a sense of equilibrium. Others teach the one-Wing theory, which states that only one Wing is dominant and influences a personality. According to one-Wing theory, a person's full Enneagram Type is expressed with both the main Type and an associated wing, e.g., an Enneagram Type Two could be 2w1 (a Type Two with a One Wing) or a 2w3 (a Type Two with a Three Wing).

WHICH THEORY IS CORRECT?

The American Journal of Psychiatry signals validity for both theories: "Individuals are generally more influenced by one Wing than the other, although traits from both wings may emerge in response to different environments. Although an individual's Wing may determine many aspects of his or her personality, the core type describes the primary motivation driving behavior"[1].

The point here isn't which theory is right or wrong, but what most resonates with you. Wings can be seen as personality flavors that you can toggle between depending on your context and level of development.

A great analogy I've heard for understanding the function and importance of the Wings is that of salt and pepper to flavor a dish. The main dish doesn't change, but adding a bit of salt and pepper elevates the taste to new heights. However, even the best meal becomes inedible if poorly done (underseasoned or overseasoned). Similarly, our Wings can flavor our personality as long as we're doing it in the right balance and at healthy levels of development.

It's essential to discover your dominant Wing, as that will give you granular details of your personality. For example, a Type Two is always empathetic, nurturing, and focused on helping others, but if their dominant Wing is One, then this individual will integrate a strong moral compass and principled integrity into their personality. As a result, the 2w1 will come across as someone with a stronger sense of duty. Their helping and nurturing nature may be directed toward community building and advocating for social justice issues instead of just focusing on their immediate loved ones. In comparison, a type Two with a dominant Three Wing will come across as more ambitious than usual. The 2w3 is less concerned about morality and instead emphasizes traits like confidence and competency. This individual may not be as oriented around service and community as the other 2w1 individual. Rather, the 2w3 will be more concerned about their image. Don't get me wrong, their goals and nurturing qualities are still the same. They will still work on fulfilling other people's desires to get what they want. But in behavioral observation, you'll see a difference in how they react to various situations and what they focus on most.

BRIEF DESCRIPTION OF THE 18 ENNEAGRAM TYPES WITH WINGS

All Enneagram Types have Wings; as in the example above, each Type will display additional flavors and focus on certain things depending on which Wing is most dominant. Here's an overview of how each Type would show up under the influence of their Wings.

1w9: Calm, practical, and meticulous perfectionist with a knack for catching inconsistencies in other people's reasoning and judgment. This individual is a deep listener and tends to easily get people to open up and trust them.

1w2: Socially aware activists and advocates who work tirelessly behind the scenes to uphold safety standards for others.

2w1: Deeply empathetic and caring with strong moral principles and integrity. This person finds fulfillment in other people's happiness and well-being.

2w3: Socially outgoing; loves to look good and be around people. This person is a great organizer and connecter of people.

3w2: Socially savvy, charming, and popular go-getter who enjoys meeting new people and networking at events.

3w4: Charismatic, attractive, driven, and organized; the boss who is always on the go with new business ideas and projects. This individual finds great joy in rewards and being efficient.

4w3: Charming, individualistic, and artistic, with a sense of wonder about the underlying beauty in nature, as well as the spectrum of human emotions.

4w5: Intense, curious, and artistic. Constantly creating and seeking to use their self-expression to highlight the universality of the human condition.

5w4: Deep, intense, and idiosyncratic. This individual values autonomy, self-reliance, and mastery of a subject. They mostly enjoy being on their own and are highly creative and a little romantic deep down.

5w6: Deep, intense, detached, and voracious researcher who gains energy from digging into fascinating topics under the radar.

6w5: Resourceful and dutiful team worker who values security and knowledge. This person tends to have a great sense of humor as well.

6w7: Optimistic and fun-loving, this individual loves exploring life but still seeks safety and comfort, which often creates contradiction and confusion.

7w6: The experience junkie who is ever-optimistic, energetic, and always searching for new projects to undertake.

7w8: Bold, creative, and often entrepreneurial, who enjoys experimenting, taking new risks, and creating with new mediums and ideas.

8w7: Headstrong, confident self-starter who loves to work hard and play hard; typically has a fearless attitude.

8w9: Confident servant leader who keeps other people's best interests (especially of those under their care) in mind to preserve harmony. This individual is more gentle and encouraging toward others.

9w8: Calm, independent vagabond on a quiet mission to discover what makes society a kinder, more accepting place.

9w1: Calm, collected, and pragmatic. This individual values cooperation and justice and the feeling of being connected to others in their community.

WHAT ARE SUB-TYPES?

Instinctual sub-types, or instinctual variants as they are also known, combine your core Enneagram Type and your instinct. What do we mean when we say instinct? Simply put, it is your survival mechanism. We are all wired in a particular way, and although there are three fundamental instincts or life forces within each of us, they are stacked differently. The order in which they are stacked, i.e., from the most dominant to the least dominant, influences our actions, thoughts, and feelings. How we navigate the demands of life is based on our sub-type.

What are the three instincts?

Claudio Naranjo teaches that we all have these three instincts. As you read through the following descriptions, try to become aware of which one shows up most in your personality and which one feels the most active in your personality. The dominant instinct is usually the one a person will feel most resonance with. They might feel neutral about their second instinct, and the third will be totally repressed or underdeveloped.

Self-preservation:

Self-preservation (SP) is one of the three basic sub-types. This variant is mainly concerned with safety, security, comfort, and, yes, self-preservation. People with a dominant self-preservation instinct prioritize the basics of life, e.g., food, shelter, family relationships, and tending to their physical and mental well-being. Energy and resource management is essential to such people, and they typically seek to avoid stressors in life or anything that could jeopardize their well-being.

Social:

Social (SO) Instinct is concerned with relationships and a sense of belonging to a group or community. People with a dominant Social Instinct tend to be socially aware and care more about the greater good above personal needs and desires. They know their place in a group, how they're perceived, and who they need to befriend. Such people find their most joy in teams or group settings where people work toward a shared purpose or common goal for the greater good. This instinct values connection and feeling involved with others.

One-to-One:

One-to-One, also referred to as Sexual (SX) instinct, is driven mainly by relationships (whether romantic or platonic) and experiencing life to the fullest. People with a dominant one-to-one instinctual variant value passion, excitement, and intimacy. They possess strong energy and actively seek out experiences where they can build bonds. With the One-to-One instinct, relationship building involves individuals, not groups or communities as with Social Instinct.

In total, adding the layers of the instinctual variants produces 27 subtypes which you'll learn about for each Enneagram type in subsequent chapters. If this all seems too overwhelming to grasp, think about the three instincts through the lens of the Centers of Intelligence. The Self-Preservation Instinct can be associated with the Head center; the One-to-One with the Body center; the Social Instinct with the Heart center. And now you must be wondering what that even means, so let's uncover that mystery next.

THE THREE CENTERS OF INTELLIGENCE

As you do the inner work and identify your true self, you'll notice that even if you type the same as another person, you'll never be identical. In fact, you may come across an individual who is the same Enneagram Type as you, yet is drastically different in their outlook and behavior. Aside from the fact that they might be leaning on a different wing than yourself, we need to consider how their instinctual variant influences their core type. But, to fully grasp the power and implications of that last statement, we'll need to discuss what the centers of intelligence are.

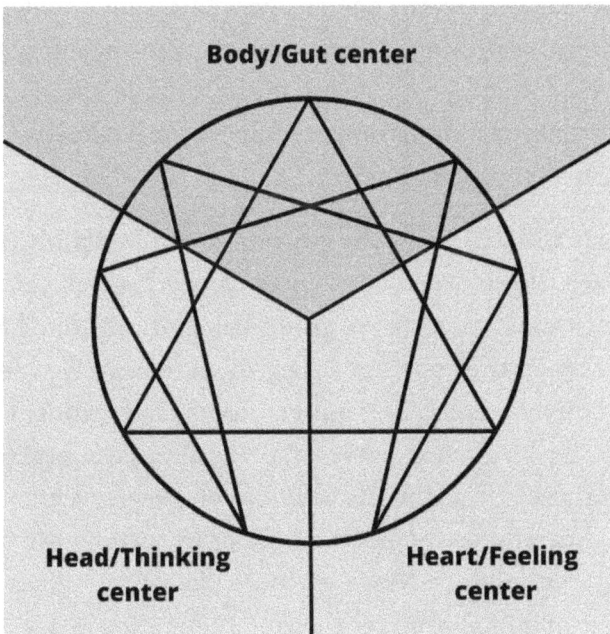

Some teachers like to call these centers of intelligence "the Triad" because they split the nine points into three equal portions, as shown in the illustration. They are the head, body, and heart, each of which provides us with basic skills that we need to navigate life and solve problems. They also indicate the underlying emotional issues that might cause us to behave in specific ways.

The head, also known as the thinking center, is more driven by logic, analysis of information, and deep thinking. Types 5, 6, and 7 make up the head center. Head types tend to be perceptive, creative, and thoughtful when operating at healthy expression levels. They are naturally good at performing cognitive tasks like visualization and imagination. However, if operating at unhealthy levels, fear is the primary underlying emotion that cripples their mind. This fear can wreak havoc if left unchecked. Unhealthy Fives react to anxiety by isolating themselves and retreating into their own minds. Sixes cope by imagining all the worst-case scenarios for everything. Sevens tend to turn their fear outward by actively running toward uncomfortable scenarios and reframing them as something exciting or adventurous—this is their way to escape their anxiety.

The body is also known as the gut center, and is mainly driven by physical sensations. The body center comprises Types 8, 9, and 1. These types are strong, stable, grounded, and connected with life, especially when they operate at healthy levels. Body types like to exert control over their environment and be independent. If operating at unhealthy levels, however, these Types can get consumed by their unchecked anger and may unconsciously act on it negatively. Eights tend to project their anger by lashing out at others when anger is building. Nines are more likely to suppress or reject their anger and hide it under the rug, pretending it doesn't exist. Types Ones deal with their unresolved anger issues by internalizing them, which often makes them overly self-critical. Unlike the other types, Ones will become aware of their anger and attempt to channel it in ways that are often unhealthy for themselves and others.

The heart is the emotional center and is mainly driven by feelings and a strong desire to connect. The feeling center is made of Types 2, 3, and 4. These types are caring, authentic, sensitive to emotional reactions, and connected with others. They love being appreciated and affirmed by others, whether they are aware of this tendency or not. The unresolved emotional issue that this group needs to resolve is shame, and it tends to subconsciously impact each Type in different ways. Type Twos are likely to express shame externally by overextending themselves in acts of service for other people so they can receive praise and affection. Threes may throw themselves into their work to be successful and receive admiration from others, and are more likely to be in denial of their shame. Type Fours attempt to control their shame by emphasizing their uniqueness to receive validation from others.

We all have one dominant Center of Intelligence; however, as with everything else you have learned so far, that doesn't mean the others are not active. We all have the head, body, and heart centers, but we often default to a favorite one that's dominant to our specific Enneagram Type. By identifying your Enneagram type, you will see which group you fall into and what dominant unresolved emotion you will need to consciously work on.

Don't be alarmed by the complexity of the various layers we've uncovered in this chapter. Your intention should be to increase your awareness and notice where you experience most resonance as more details are expressed for each Enneagram type. Trust in this process, and know that as we diver deeper into each Type in upcoming chapters, you'll gain more clarity, and things will start clicking into place.

THE DEEPER PURPOSE OF THE ENNEAGRAM

The real gift of the Enneagram tool is its ability to invite us to ponder and observe the mystery of our true identity. It initiates a process of inquiry that can lead us to a more profound truth about ourselves and our place in the world. If you discover your Type and use it as a scapegoat, as I've observed with a few people who say, "Of course I am critical of everything! After all, I'm a One," or "You know how we Sevens are! Commitment is really not my thing," then we're simply justifying our behavior instead of recognizing our blind spots and areas of growth and expansion. Any time you use your Enneagram tool to rigidly lock yourself into a limiting behavior, you're missing the purpose of this tool. Knowing your Type is important, but it's only valuable if you're using it as the kick-off point of your quest for self-discovery. Your true self can only be found beyond the traits of your Enneagram type. Your aim, and mine, is to do the inner work so we can stop automatic reactions of our personality. We want to approach life and relationships from a higher place than mere personality. The more awareness, insight, and clarity we bring to the mechanisms of our personality, the easier it will be to discover our true Selves. And that is the real purpose of the Enneagram. Head over to the resource section for the online Enneagram test I recommend.

---

1. https://psychiatryonline.org/doi/full/10.1176/appi.ajp-rj.2020.150301

CHAPTER 3

CULTIVATING AWARENESS AND UNDERSTANDING THE 9 PASSIONS

During the introduction and brief history of the Enneagram symbol and personality types, we mentioned the seven deadly sins or passions that Ichazo referenced to develop the modern-day Enneagram. In this chapter and the next, we'll investigate what these terms mean and why they matter to your quest for self-discovery. Before that, let's discuss one of the most critical qualities you must cultivate - self-awareness.

CULTIVATING AWARENESS

It is true that understanding the Enneagram personality types profoundly and with great clarity is a pre-requisite for transformation. But information alone doesn't bring about change. As William Shakespear once wrote in The Merchant of Venice, "If to do were as easy as to know what we're good to do, chapels had been churches, and poor men's cottaged princes' palaces. It is a good divine that follows his own instructions: I can easier teach twenty what were good to be done, than be one of the twenty to follow mine own teaching." In other words, it takes more than just learning about the Enneagram to transform your life. Most students of personal development struggle to experience new results because they cannot transfer the learned material into everyday living. It's easy to be calm, positive, and think abundance in a workshop or a weekend retreat by the lakeside. But that doesn't guarantee that you'll finally change your life. None of us can will or think or technique our way into transformation. The kind of progress and success we dream of doesn't happen automatically, just because you pick up a book such as this or sign up for a masterclass. Active participation on a consistent daily basis is necessary. Without it, no lasting transformation can occur. So how do you ensure that everything you learn about the Enneagram positively transforms your life forever? How can you shift from intellectual recognition of Truth to living it as a way of life now and always? By cultivating more awareness in your life. The Enneagram will empower you to let go of the limiting mechanisms of your personality so that you can experience more deeply who and what you really are. And you need a tremendous amount of self-awareness to catch yourself moment by moment. As you consciously and intentionally participate in the living of your Truth, that practice will lead to permanent transformation.

Why is self-awareness critical in this quest for self-discovery?

A simple agreed-upon definition of self-awareness is "the ability to observe oneself clearly and objectively through reflection and introspection." In other words, it's about monitoring our inner worlds, thoughts, emotions, and beliefs. According to most sacred traditions around the world, observing ourselves and being vigilant as we interact with the world is one of the most powerful things we can do to gain mastery in life. It is the path to our full awakening to who we really are and realizing that we are more than just physical beings living in a three-dimensional world. As we awaken, we become more aware and learn to "catch ourselves in the act" as we behave according to our personality and conditioning. When we are able to notice what we are doing in the moment, and we are willing to experience our current state completely, without judgment, that's when the magic happens.

On the quest for self-discovery, awareness is vitally important because it enables us to see our habits and conditions more clearly as they occur. And when we can see them in action, those old patterns move from the subconscious, where we have no control over them, to the conscious mind, where we can dissolve and alter them. Analyzing past behavior is helpful, but can never be as powerful as present moment observation. Let me share a story to illustrate this point. I once caught myself in a moment when I was about to enter a heated argument with my girlfriend. At the time, this inner work was still pretty new to me, and we'd only been dating a few months. She said something that triggered some disturbing emotions, and I felt my entire body shift into a different state. Ordinarily, I would have fallen into the trap of arguing, but this was the first time I observed myself and witnessed the sensations in my body, the brewing negativity, and that urge to lash out. It was such an incredible experience because, in that moment of awareness, I realized that I didn't really want to get into an argument and mess up our weekend getaway. I saw that my reaction was just a way to justify something deeper. So, instead, I began to question what was really behind that behavior. What was this important point that I wanted to make, or what was it I was trying to defend and hide? Becoming more curious about myself completely dissipated the situation and resulted in me taking a step back and heading out for a long meditative stroll that revealed a lot more about my approach to romantic relationships. The trick, though, is that I was able to observe without judgment; I was able to stay in that discomfort long enough to question and meet my feelings with curiosity rather than shrink into embarrassment. Then I applied some mindfulness practices that work for my Type—we'll talk more about all these practices for each of the Enneagram types.

The more self-awareness you cultivate, the easier it will be to observe and catch yourself in the moment, enabling you to make different choices. It will also increase your ability to regulate emotions. At first, it might feel embarrassing and uncomfortable; you might have a strong urge to shut down or distract yourself from facing those unwanted sensations, but if you can just stay present and embrace that discomfort, you'll notice something new emerging. With patience and a lot of self-acceptance, you'll start to experience self-compassion and understanding that transcends your personality. That's when you begin to tap into the real you. That's when you begin to awaken.

A Course in Miracles writes, "The Bible says that a deep sleep fell upon Adam, and nowhere is there a reference to his waking up." Gurdjieff and many other spiritual teachers have often asserted that our current normal state is akin to being asleep, at least from the soul's perspective. That sounds strange for someone new to inner work because it's hard to convince your ego as you read this that you're asleep. But what if I told you that there are many levels of awareness? Consider how "real" a dream feels when you're being chased by an animal. Your physiology responds as though you were awake, yet your body in this reality is wholly immobilized on your bed as you dream. Would it be too ridiculous to open up to the possibility that, even at this moment, you could be asleep in relation to other levels of awareness or higher realities? In this current level of awareness, your personality and ego tend to have the most control. They dominate your day and determine your behavior. However, through practice and cultivating more awareness, you could bridge a gap between your personality and a higher version of yourself that remains unseen and unknown. Waking up from the trance of personality and being able to detach yourself from that version of yourself that's driven by impulse, desire, and emotions reveals a you that you might have been seeking since childhood. So this isn't about villainizing your personality; instead, it's about giving you the power to choose how you'll show up in any given moment. Most of us, especially our political leaders, run around in life being led by a mischievous six-year-old. Is it any wonder we are continually recreating drama and chaos? Once we understand, however, the mechanisms of personality, and begin to identify who we really are independent of personality, the game of life takes on new meaning. As we recognize that we are a Type Five or a Type Eight, we're not enslaved by that Fiveness or Eightness. Instead, we can choose at any given moment how to direct our Type, and when we see that it doesn't serve us, we have the choice to override it altogether. Once you begin practicing more self-awareness, you're ready to face your greatest teacher: your Type's passion.

THE 9 PASSIONS

In the context of the modern Enneagram system for personality typing, Ichazo traced early ideas about the ancient "Nine Divine Attributes" from Greece to the desert fathers of the fourth century who first developed the concept of the Seven Deadly Sins (basically the opposite or distortions of the Divine Attributes) and incorporated them into our modern system. Although Christian tradition talked about the Seven Deadly Sins at first, two others were later added: fear and deceit. Ichazo's teaching of the Passions in the context of the Enneagram model that we use tells us we all have each of these "Passions" within us. However, depending on our Enneagram Type, a particular passion will be more pronounced. That's the passion that shows up repeatedly throughout our lives and is the root of our imbalance in life. It distorts and traps our ego in unconstructive ways as it tries to resolve that deep-seated issue.

The idea of the Deadly Sins, aka the Passions, will make more sense if you think of the sin in the following way. Sin means to "miss the mark," but not as most religions teach (something bad or evil). So the 9 Passions represent the nine main ways that we lose our center and become distorted in our thoughts, feelings, and actions.

Passion for type 1: *Anger*
Passion for type 2: *Pride*
Passion for type 3: *Deceit*
Passion for type 4: *Envy*
Passion for type 5: *Avarice*
Passion for type 6: *Fear*
Passion for type 7: *Gluttony*
Passion for type 8: *Lust*
Passion for type 9: *Sloth*

Each of these Passions is discussed in detail under their corresponding Enneagram Type in subsequent chapters. As mentioned before, your passion is your greatest teacher. When you recognize this underlying emotional reaction and how it plays out in your life, you will finally start moving toward your genuine desire in life and your essential nature. What is your essential nature? Great question. Let's unpack that next.

CHAPTER 4

ESSENCE PERSONALITY EGO

A t this point in your quest, you ought to be realizing that while your personality matters, it's not who you are. If you've already landed on that Truth, congratulations. Life is about to get way more intriguing and wonderful. The fundamental Truth of Life is that we are far more than the familiar conditioned concepts we call personality. Our true potential is grand and remains mostly dormant and untapped until we begin this quest of self-discovery. Beyond the accepted limitations of our ego-personality, each of us is a magnificent being. Deepak Chopra likes to refer to this being as our Higher Self. I like that term, so from now on, whenever I desire to make a distinction between your ego personality and True Self, I shall refer to them as the ego self and the Higher Self. The Higher Self cannot be seen, tasted, touched, or analyzed by the logical mind, but there is a simple way to "experience" your Higher Self.

How can you begin to discern the difference between the Higher Self and the ego-self?

- The Higher Self is always certain and clear about things. Your ego-self is influenced by countless outside influences, which creates confusion.
- The Higher Self is always at peace. Your ego-self is restless, agitated, and easily disturbed.
- The Higher Self is stable. Your ego self shifts constantly.
- The Higher Self is love. Your ego self, lacking love, seeks it from external sources, including people and things.

At this moment, while reading the words in this book, become aware that you're reading. Notice yourself and your thoughts as you reflect on my words. Now, ask yourself, "Who is noticing that I am reading?"

If you can sit in self-contemplation with that thought, you'll come to experience the quality of Being or Presence of the observer, aka your Higher Self. Your Higher Self is ever-present in the moment, and is what Enneagram experts call your "Essence." In spiritual language, this Essence is often referred to as the spark of the Divine that rests within. As mentioned before in *A Course in Miracles*, the human race fell into a deep sleep since the time of Adam, and in that sleep, we forgot our true nature. Here's how I've come to understand this teaching. My Higher Self is the Divine spark, the real and powerful me. My ego-self is the everyday little me formed due to my beliefs, culture, childhood, societal norms, and environment. It's the human conditioning aspect of myself that I've grown to believe is who I am. The more I go through life living only from the perspective of my ego-personality self, the more distant and disconnected I am from my Higher Self, and that's where all the problems stem from. That disconnect breeds the restlessness, void, loneliness, fear, and lack that I try to grapple with in my physical world by chasing after things and people, hoping that will finally solve my internal issues. In this "darkness," I do not experience my own Divine nature and certainly cannot perceive divinity in anything or anyone else. Instead, I get trapped in whatever perspective my ego-personality holds true.

Notice what thoughts, emotions, and beliefs came up for you as you read that last paragraph. Hearing these things for the first time is entirely foreign for many of us, so it's easy for your ego to reject these ideas. I only ask that you suspend unbelief and keep an open mind until you've gone through the entire book. Then you can choose what you want to believe and live by. In normal everyday living, we don't experience our Essence and its many aspects because our awareness is dominated by ego-personality. As we learn to cultivate the awareness discussed in chapter 4 and become aware of ourselves moment-by-moment, it becomes more apparent that there's more to us than our personality and impulses. And in those moments, we can catch glimpses of our Essence. To be clear, reconnecting with your Essence doesn't kill your personality or destroy your ego; you will still function as a human being in the world, but you will do so above ordinary levels of human awareness because you'll have direct contact with Divinity.

This quest is, therefore, one of remembering. It's remembering who you really are and the magnificence within you. It's about returning to your True Self. The Enneagram's purpose is to guide you on this journey of awakening. It's here to give you insights into your specific psychological and spiritual makeup, not so that you can comfortably fit into a particular category, but so you can become aware of the many ways you're limiting your Higher Self through the expressions of your limited personality. Many people think the Enneagram is meant to justify their behaviors or provide them with consolation for being of a particular nature. This is far from the truth. The Enneagram tool wasn't created to place us in a box, but instead to show us the box we are already in and provide a way out. So, if you want out of your old way of living and into something profoundly different and more aligned with your true Essence, rest easy because you have to take that first step today.

SHOULD WE GET RID OF OUR PERSONALITIES?

Most people assume that returning to one's Essence means abandoning or rejecting the personality and ego. This is misinformation and certainly not what the Enneagram teaches. We don't want to villainize or even eliminate the ego-personality because we need it to enjoy and function in human living. So if you've been fearful about losing your identity or becoming less functional in society, don't be. The Enneagram teaches us to get in touch with our Essence and reconnect with our True Self so we can become whole. Wholeness includes and integrates all aspects, including personality. Think about the restlessness, fear, instability, and lack of lack that plagues our ego-personality. The quest for self-discovery and reconnecting finally heals all those issues because our ego can finally receive permanent, unconditional love, strength, stability, and a sense of power that it could not access anywhere else. That transforms our ego-personality from unhealthy levels to the healthiest and most productive version because it's nourished directly from the Divinity within us. Moments of "flow" and peak performance are typically the result of an individual who has become present and aware, aligned with their True Self. In such states, the activity at hand becomes more enjoyable and yields better results.

The solution, therefore, is not to reject our personality but rather to see it for what it really is: a tiny part of who we are in totality. The personality still exists, but there is a more active intelligence, a higher, more powerful presence underlying that personality that is in charge and on the driver's seat of our lives. We shift from a personality identity to an Essence identity. That makes all the difference in our human experience.

How quickly can we make this shift?

It would be inaccurate to claim that you will switch from ego-personality identity to Higher Self identity at the snap of a finger, or that it's a one-time thing that lasts forever. The Truth is, this is an ongoing process that you work on moment-by-moment. With practice, you move further away from the lower levels of awareness to the higher levels. Each moment of self-realization will transform you to some degree, and the more you pile on these moments, the higher you rise until, soon enough, your default expression will be an expanded awareness. As you progress and practice, your identity gradually opens up to include more of your Higher Self. In other words, your inner light and essential nature will shine brighter day by day as you keep doing the work. As long as you never stop working to improve, you will continue to experience deeper, higher, and more profound divine self-expression beyond anything you can imagine.

BASIC DRIVES OF THE PERSONALITY

Before we dive deep into each personality type, let's bring a little more clarity to the fundamental mechanisms that drive the personality. These are basic fear and basic desire.

The basic fear is rooted in a sense of loss that each personality feels consciously or unconsciously. It comes from the loss of contact with our Essential nature in early childhood. Even children born under the best circumstances will not have all their developmental needs perfectly met, no matter how well-intentioned their parents are. For various reasons, parents will at times have difficulty coping with all the needs of their babies (especially in areas they also lacked as children). For example, if an infant expresses joyfulness and delight in being alive, but her mother is depressed, it's unlikely the mother will be comfortable with or even encourage the baby's joy. As a result, the baby learns to suppress her happiness to keep her mother from getting more upset. There are many learned behaviors that, as children, we adopted to enable us to either fit in or protect our caregivers based on observed behavior. Some children contract and suppress their emotions entirely; others go to the other extreme to get a reaction from their caregiver. But in all cases, our conditioned environment always hampers our true and fullest expression in one way or another. We react in ways that correspond to our forming personality depending on our temperament. As we continue to grow in our formative years, our unmet needs and subsequent blockages pile on, and we become keenly aware of a disconnect. Something feels off, and that creates deep-seated anxiety and fear regardless of personality type. Each Type has its own characteristic basic fear. Even if we cannot express it in words, we feel the tug of powerful, unconscious fear and anxiety, especially when under the pressures of life. Keep in mind that part of what drives our basic fear is our ego-personality's fear of nothingness, which is pretty much a universal paradigm. As you go through each of the nine types, you'll recognize that all these fears are present in you to some extent, but your own Type's basic fear will stand out much more than the others. Here's an example to show you what I mean.

EXERCISE 1:

Read the following sentences and notice which one stands out most (maybe even stirs up painful flashbacks or makes you cringe).

#1: It's not okay to make mistakes.

#2: It's not okay to you have your own needs. Don't be selfish.

#3: It's not okay to have your own feelings and identity.

#4: It's not okay to be too happy or too functional.

#5: It's not okay to be comfortable in the world.

#6: It's not okay to trust yourself.

#7: It's not okay to depend on anyone for anything.

#8: It's not okay to be vulnerable or trust anyone.

#9: It's not okay to assert yourself.

Which of these statements really pressed hard on your psyche?

Take note of whatever insights come to you. For now, let's keep exploring.

We talked about Basic Fear and the fact that it arises from a deep sense of disconnect from our Essence nature. Now let's talk about Basic Desire because it's equally important to understand where that's rooted as well.

Basic desire arises as the defense mechanism to counteract that sense of loss and disconnect that our basic fear generates within. It is the ego's way of "handling the situation and making things okay." I like to imagine the ego-self regularly thinks to himself, "If I can just get X, that feeling/void/restlessness/emptiness/loss that we're experiencing will be gone, and I can finally feel whole again." X represents whatever your specific personality type struggles with the most. It could be love, security, peace, and so forth. Many Enneagram teachers refer to the Basic Desire as the "ego agenda" because it's basically what the ego is always striving after. But here's the thing. No one says your ego desires are wrong. In fact, when you dig deeper, they are pointing you to something wonderful and right. The ego just mainly focuses on surface-level humanistic needs. Unfortunately, the ego tends to fixate too much on its specific basic desire to the point of neglect of other human and spiritual needs. Things tend to go wrong when we attempt to fulfill our basic desire in misguided ways. Suppose you are the personality type that is ever-seeking and obsessing over security. Perhaps, you always want to feel safe and secure in everything in your life. In an uncertain world where change is constant, attaining that aim is challenging from an ego perspective. Maybe it has caused you to push too hard to the point where you start self-sabotaging and ruining even the same security your ego needs. As you will see in upcoming chapters when we talk about the Enneagram Type Six, this is a common experience for Sixes operating at lower levels of development. Similarly, each personality type is capable of such self-sabotaging behavior, which, ironically, robs them of the very thing they are chasing after.

Look around the world today. Thanks to technology, the Internet, and social media, we are more connected than ever. And yet, more people claim loneliness and the inability to find their soul mate. There are more divorce cases than ever, and people even take their own lives due to lacking love in their lives. That is the sad outcome when individuals chase after their basic desires in misguided ways. And when that happens, our basic desire turns into a fixation that unwittingly blocks our Essential nature creating a wider gap between our everyday self and our Higher Self. The irony here is that when we are fixated on our basic desire, our personality craves control. It will not relinquish that control until it believes the desire has been fully and permanently attained. Unfortunately, as you might have already experienced, any goal achievement doesn't guarantee the feeling of wholeness or completion. How often have you chased after a money goal thinking it will make you feel rich, only to achieve it and still feel poor and unhappy? Or perhaps it was a romantic partner that you chased after, thinking they would fill a void, yet a few months or years in, that same void persisted?

Going back to our example of the Type Six who relentlessly seeks security in all the wrong ways. That individual would want to control everything in their world, and they wouldn't allow themselves to relax and become present until they feel their world is completely secure. As we know, without Presence, there is no return to the Essential nature. So, of course, that person will feel trapped in a cycle of anxiety and insecurity, trying hard to control the external world and force things to feel stable and secure. Understanding this, can you see the interrelation between the basic fear and basic desire? Are you seeing why most teachers say that human nature is driven by fear and desire? In this construct, we can summarize that our personality operates on a model of fleeing from our basic fear and pursuing our basic desire. The entire feeling-tone of our character emerges out of this dynamic, and it becomes the underlying drive for our ego and sense of self.

Time for another exercise to move you deeper into this quest. In the previous exercise, we focused on statements that would enable you to notice your most prominent basic fear. This time, we're focused on statements that can help you identify your basic desire.

EXERCISE 2:

#1: I need to live in integrity and do what's right. I operate with a strong moral code, and so should everyone else.
#2: I need to be loved and needed by others.
#3: I must become and show that I am valuable and prove to others that I deserve admiration.

#4: I must find my true identity and express my uniqueness to the world.

#5: I need to be competent and the most knowledgeable so I can know Truth.

#6: I need to be secure.

#7: I must be happy all the time.

#8: I need to protect myself from the world and show that I am strong at all times.

#9: I need to find peace in my mind and life at all costs.

After going through this second exercise, can you find a statement of desire, and does it correspond with or match the basic fear that most stood out for you?

The answer you give is already enlightening you on your Enneagram type and also the area of your life where growth seeks to happen. As Andrew Harvey once said, "The very things we wish to avoid, neglect and flee from turn out to be the 'prima materia' from which all real growth comes."

Ready for real growth? It's time to learn about your Enneagram type.

SECTION 11

THE 9 TYPES

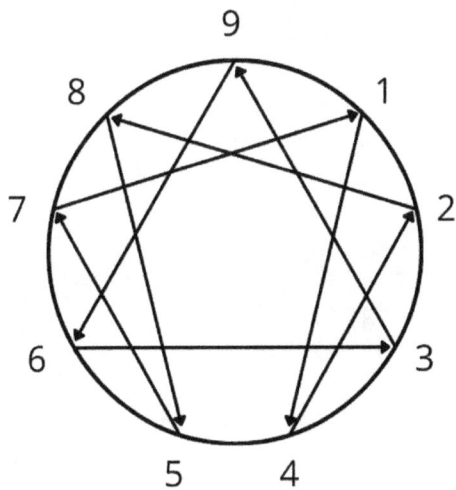

CHAPTER 5

ENNEAGRAM TYPE 1

THE REFORMER OR PERFECTIONIST

T his chapter and the next will go in-depth on the Enneagram Type One, commonly referred to as the reformer or perfectionist. The title - reformer is a perfect fit for this enneatype because these individuals thrive when they're changing the world around them for the better. Type Ones are idealistic, purposeful, self-controlled, and highly conscientious. They adhere to strict moral and ethical codes and operate with extremely high standards. Because they desire to make everything around them "right" by their standards, they can easily create friction and resistance when interacting with others. Enneagram Type Ones fall into the Gut or Body Center, making anger one of the main emotions that hinder personal growth and evolution, especially if unresolved.

Many Ones who aren't yet operating at the higher and healthier levels of development often fall into habits of criticism, judgment, and perfectionism. But here's the thing. These great expectations of perfection (as unrealistic as they might be) aren't just placed on others. Ones tend to set exceptionally high standards for themselves, causing them to live in constant self-criticism. Their strong inner critic takes the driver's seat, which dictates how they behave and treat others. From an outside observer, Type Ones might be great at execution, planning, organization, and promoting positive change, but they're also difficult to work with, impossible to please, and in some cases, total jerks.

STRENGTHS OF A ONE:

Ones are great at getting things done, and they don't allow anyone to stand in their way or hold them back. They often make incredible change-makers, crusaders, teachers, and activists.

Ones are also capable of self-leading and efficiently solving setbacks and problems that arise as they pursue their goals.

A defining strength for type One is their ability to go the extra mile to ensure a project or situation is handled exceptionally well. They will stop at nothing to attain perfection.

Due to their idealistic worldview and the need to get everything done right, they pay close attention to details, fuss over the little things and never take shortcuts. That makes this type extremely diligent, hardworking, and reliable.

Key personality traits of Type One

- Focused and purposeful.
- A compulsive need to be right all the time.
- Meritocracy and organization.
- Hard working.
- Being good or perfect.
- Politeness.

Common hobbies for a Type One

- Organizing
- Fundraising
- Tutoring
- Planning

FEARS AND WEAKNESSES

By now, it's evident that one of the distinguishing expressions of a Type One is the need to live by very high moral standards and do things the right way. That comes from the need to be good and to be perceived as good and worthy.

What's the Basic Fear driving this behavior? The fear of being bad, corrupt, evil, or defective.

As a type One, you may fear being misinterpreted, accused, blamed, or considered fraud for not living up to the high standards you've set. The idea that others may not see you as perfect is unbearable because that will mean you're imperfect and therefore defective. In a more practical sense, you are fussy about your physical space and how messy others make it. You fuss over unclear projects or when a loved one acts recklessly. If expectations are unclear and there's a lack of quality in any area, you will lose your mind. For example, a businessman who once attended our virtual meetups shared that whenever he walks into the office if even a single light bulb is off, he loses his mind because it's unacceptable that his office manager would call themselves a professional when they can barely tend to office duties. This is a great example of how detail-oriented and perfectionistic Ones can be. Deep down, it's all about the need to be good and perfect. Instead of criticizing yourself over this habit of perfectionism in a world that's anything but perfect all the time, it's better to get curious about why that fear is prevailing.

Perhaps somewhere during your upbringing, you may have picked up the message that you need to be perfect all the time? You're an idealist at heart, so it makes sense that anything flawed should be fixed immediately, including you.

How does this Basic Fear often manifest itself?

You will often see and catch even the tiniest mistakes in others as you interact with them. If it's in your social life, you may stop dating someone or decline an invitation simply because they didn't live up to the details of your ideal. At work, it might show up as constantly getting into conflict with work colleagues over how something should be done and why your idea is the right way to solve certain challenges. But it doesn't stop there. By far, the biggest issue for a One is the ongoing negative chatter in their mind. It feels almost impossible to tame that inner critic who seems impossible to please. You might become resentful and angry with yourself, others, or a less than ideal situation that throws you off your game. And because you're a body-based type, dealing with feelings (especially anger) isn't a strong suit, so you're likely to suppress emotions that typically leak out in the most unhealthy ways. We'll study different levels of development so you can start identifying where you are on your journey and how to move toward the most connected and healthy version of yourself. But first, let's take a look at your Basic desire and motivations.

DESIRES AND MOTIVATIONS

The Basic Desire for a Type One is to be good and honorable. If you identify as a Type One, there are a few key things to recognize about your personality. First off, leading a purposeful life is extremely important to you, which is praiseworthy. The best way to rise into higher levels of development is to align your goals and work choices with your purpose. People call you a perfectionist or bossy mainly because they don't fully understand how important it is to you that things get done the proper way. Attaining the best in every outcome isn't just a slogan for you. It's part of your personality's DNA, and it's okay to honor that as long as it doesn't enslave you. As a type One, you're extremely responsible and pragmatic and strive to make the world a better place. You rely on your judgment to come up with solutions and do a great job separating emotions from facts so you don't get overwhelmed by emotions like other types. Ethics is also a big issue for you. In fact, as we break down your core values, you'll notice how connected they are and why all are necessary for enabling you to live an honorable life. Let's name the top values your personality identifies with most.

Core values

As a type One, these are some of the core values you may hold dear.

- Integrity
- Honesty
- Ethics
- Duty
- Humility
- Organization, structure
- Cleanliness, tidiness, order
- Service above self

Type One celebrities and famous people you might know include Apple co-founder Steve Jobs, Canadian Singer Celine Dion,

Actress Julie Andrews, Actress Natalie Portman, Anti-colonial nationalist and political ethicist Mahatma Gandhi, and the former first lady of the United States, Michelle Obama.

Wondering if you could be a type One? Here are some personality indicators:

1. You hold yourself to very high standards. Some might even say unrealistically high standards.
2. You are a stickler for rules. You always need clarity about what others expect of you and what the boundaries are so you can act accordingly.
3. You exercise high levels of self-restraint and work hard to civilize your natural instincts. That makes you more rational and less impulsive.
4. You care a lot about making a difference in the world and doing your part to make things better for yourself and others.
5. As a child, you may have taken on a lot of responsibility, turning you into the "dependable one" that everyone relies on. People know they can count on you no matter what because you always keep your word and take your duties very seriously. However, this comes with a dark side as well because it means you carry a heavy burden all your life.
6. You have a strong inner critic that judges every action you take. That voice is behind your constant need for perfection in your world. Left unchecked, this voice can be the cause of great anxiety, self-criticism, and self-doubt.
7. You're utterly frustrated at how sloppy and subpar most people are. Because you strive so hard for perfection and

work hard to live with integrity, you can't stand it when others act recklessly or neglect their duties.

8. You have a hard time relaxing and just allowing yourself to be a little spontaneous.

9. Being corrupted, evil, or betraying your moral code is simply unacceptable.

10. You worry that expressing the anger that sometimes brews inside you or allowing yourself to just explode emotionally will cause you to fall from the ideals and standards you've set for yourself. So rather than express your negative emotions, you prefer to hold in your anger and repress it under clenched fists, a tight jawbone, and gritted teeth.

11. Friends and family members may call you overly critical, a bit of a pushover, and too strict if they were asked to describe you. But you don't mind because you know that's what it takes to create the kind of success you desire.

YOUR WINGS

Wings are the numbers that reside directly on the two sides of your Enneagram Type. As an enneatype One, you have -

- The Enneagram One with Nine-Wing: "The idealist."
- The Enneagram One with Two-Wing: "The Advocate"

While you may have tendencies that lean into both wings, you'll likely be more dominant in one than the other, and this will be your dominant Wing.

Meaning of your Wing

If you're a 1w9 (One with Nine-Wing), then you will tend to be more introverted than a 1w2. You're more of that principled idealist and always think before you speak so you can avoid going against your moral code in any way. Sometimes, this leads to delays and procrastination because you just need to be sure and think everything through before acting. A strong aspect of having this Wing as the dominant of the two is that your decisions and actions are almost always failproof.

If you're a 1w2 (One with Two-Wing), then you're more extraverted and outgoing in nature. You're more empathetic and understanding of others compared to a 1w9. You feel deeply inclined to help the people around you. While you are still an excellent problem solver, you struggle a lot with striking that balance between controlling things and people and supporting them.

The Arrows and what they mean

When you look closely at the Enneagram symbol, you'll notice that there are lines within the circle connecting the personality points in the circle's perimeter. These lines aren't arbitrary. They are, in fact, arrows that map how each personality will react in certain situations. Your personality type is linked to two other points (4 and 7). One arrow indicates how you will react in stressful, pressure-filed situations or when you're feeling like your back is up against the wall. It explains the actions or reactions of an unhealthy personality. In Enneagram terminology, this is called the Direction of Stress or the Direction of Disintegration. The other arrow indicates how a healthy version of your personality reacts to situations and how your personality grows in different environments. The term for this is the Direction of Growth or the Direction of Integration. In brief, moving in the direction of stress (4), you would be moody, irrational, and temperamental. However, moving in the direction of growth (7), you become more joyful, spontaneous, and relaxed like a healthy Seven.

To understand the relationship of these arrows and how we came about with healthy and unhealthy levels, let's talk about the various levels of development for type One.

LEVELS OF DEVELOPMENT

Levels of Development arise from Riso and Hudson's teachings and the founders of the Enneagram Institute, which is a great place to take your Enneagram Test. Their theory posits that all individuals fall into one of nine levels of functioning. The lowest level is nine, and the highest is level one. The levels are divided into a triad that subcategorizes these levels as healthy (1,2,3), average levels (4,5,6), and unhealthy levels (7,8,9).

Unhealthy Levels

Level 9: This level of development is the most destructive and unhealthy. Although we all go through this level during infancy when we're purely interested in our needs and nothing else, this level should be outgrown as soon as possible. As babies and infants, operating at a level 9 where you care about nothing else other than getting your way and having your needs met is perfectly normal, but this is extremely unhealthy for adults. Thus an adult One operating at this level is cruel, punitive, and condemnatory toward others. Such a Type One is likely to experience serve depression, nervous breakdowns, and even struggle with obsessive-compulsive disorders.

Level 8: This level is where a type One becomes obsessive about imperfection and the wrongdoing around them. At this level, the

One is quite delusional and compulsive. They also tend to be quite contradictory by saying one thing and then doing the opposite.

Level 7: This type One is rigid, intolerant, self-righteous, and highly dogmatic. When dealing with others who are wrong, they tend to be very severe in their judgments and unrespectful of other people's feelings or personal boundaries. At this level of development, the individual only deals in absolutes, and they alone know "The Truth ."

Average Levels

Level 6: This level of development is moving toward the path of healthy expressions but is still highly critical both of themselves and others. Such a type One will be picky, judgmental, and a classic perfectionist. They are opinionated about everything and have a knack for correcting people and tormenting them to do "the right thing" by their standards. This type One is impatient, abrasive, and constantly scolds everyone around them. At this level, type One is overcompensating and still driven by the desire to advance their ego agendas, even if it's at the cost of others.

Level 5: This level of development brings with it the expression of a lot of defensive behavior. Type One at this level is extremely afraid of making mistakes and failing to reach their ideals. Everything has to go according to their plans or lose it. This individual is more organized, orderly, and extremely hardworking. They are rigid, emotionally constricted, and highly impersonal even with people they like. Their main focus is to compulsively tend to each detail so they can achieve their goals.

Level 4: At this average level of development, there's a strong expression of imbalance for type One. The individual is becoming high-minded and quite dissatisfied with reality. They feel it's up to them to improve everything and everyone in their world, often moving them into advocates, critics, and crusaders as they attempt to tame that inner critic so they can reach their highest ideals.

Healthy Levels

Level 3: This level of development gets us into the more healthy expressions of a type One personality where they care about social values. At this point, they have outgrown purely ego-driven goals and now see their role as individuals in society and the world as a whole. This is where the ego begins to heal and operate more constructively. This type One is extremely principled and always wants to be fair, ethical, objective, and embody justice. They have a strong sense of responsibility and personal integrity.

Level 2: This level of development is attained through the commitment to doing the inner work and learning more about oneself. At this level, the Type One's ego reaches the individual's Ideal Self. This Type One is conscientious, reasonable, self-disciplined, mature, and moderate in all things. They have an intense sense of right and wrong and a purpose that drives their life.

Level 1: At this level of development, Type One reaches the holy grail of self-mastery and wholeness. This is indeed a Type One at their best and the level of true freedom. It involves facing your deepest fears and genuinely understanding yourself as both a human and spiritual being. Although you reach your ideal Self at Level Two, transcendence and enlightenment occur at this level. You become extraordinarily wise and discerning, accepting things just as they are. Your ability to discern truth and know what action to take at any given point is awe-inspiring, and you become more hopeful, calm, accepting, humane, and liberated from the inside out. This is the dream for all of us on this quest, and it is within your grasp as you continue to walk this path.

TYPE ONE'S PASSION

The Passions (also called the Deadly Sins) are our teachers. Each type has a dominant passion that can enable the individual to uncover their underlying emotional reaction and unresolved issues when recognized. By following that thread, the person becomes aware of how they've lost sight of their true desire and their essential nature.

For a type One, your Passion is Anger, although many teachers agree that a more accurate description is resentment. Anger in and of itself isn't an issue, so don't villainize the experience of this emotion. The problem is that as a type One, you tend to repress the emotion of anger which leads to continual frustration, dissatisfaction, and resentment. That breeds an inner resentment that influences how you relate to yourself and others.

Pause for a moment. Think about how often you think, feel or even speak the words, "This just isn't right. Nothing is as it should be!" If you can become aware of your Passion of Anger, you'll likely see that it results from a need to change or fix everything around you. So you end up angry with someone (or yourself) for not being good enough.

Increasing awareness of this Passion opens up a new choice. It enables you to transform and start moving toward your Essence, which returns you back to your virtue of Serenity.

CHILDHOOD AND EMOTIONAL PATTERNS OF TYPE ONE

We can now see that Anger is one of the leading emotions for type Ones and really all the types that form the Gut or Body Center. But most Ones have a hard time recognizing that they have anger and resentment issues. So to bring even more clarity so you can take appropriate action, let's talk about how you internalize this emotion and how others experience it. Because you tend to reflect your anger inwardly, it tends to leak out in the form of criticism, judgment, and scolding. And you don't just do it to others, you also do it to yourself. So unlike a type Eight who also has the Passion of Anger and tends to project it externally, you do everything possible to contain and conceal the suffering you experience. Depending on your dominant Wing Type, specific qualities will be more pronounced than others.

Type One Wing 9 - The Idealist

A type One with Wing Nine means the individual has all the qualities of a One and a few qualities of type Nine. Although you can be influenced by both Wings, the more dominant Wing will resonate deeply with you. Some of the traits of that particular Wing will be easy to identify in yourself. As you study and understand more about yourself, it is imperative to identify which Wing is more dominant and, if possible, the proportion of the Wing score if both as active. Studying your main personality and wing types can also give you a better understanding of your childhood wounds and how that's affecting your adult life. Type 1w9 is typically rational, calm, and balanced with a sense of right and wrong. There's a strong emphasis on justice and fairness, especially when dealing with people. Does that sound like you? Here are some more details of this personality:

- Loyal friend
- Extremely detail-oriented
- Improvement oriented
- Stand up for the powerless and underprivileged
- Striving to make a difference in society
- A strong code of ethics

1w9 also prefer to keep to themselves and hardly allow their emotions to show. They may have had a disconnected relationship with their caregiver during their childhood years. They likely grew up in an extreme environment - either too strict or too lenient. If the household was also a religious one, then this child probably developed a need to please an angry, capricious God. Having a dysfunctional relationship with parents and the authority figures in their environment, this child needed to create a personality that didn't express themselves emotionally to avoid evoking anger in others. They also had to learn to create a strict set of boundaries for themselves and a particular of carrying themselves in the world to preserve a spotless, flawless reputation as a child. Control had to be mastered early in life. As adults, we see it playing out in relationships, work life, and social interactions. The need to strive for perfection, maintain control, and remain vigilant and rational comes from childhood experiences.

Type 1w9 personality is extremely cautious and overly protective of their reputation in the workplace. As a 1w9, some of the best careers you can excel at include:

- Judge
- Social Worker
- Journalist
- Consultant
- Guidance Counselor
- Environmentalist
- Public Relations Specialist
- Ambassador

Being averse to criticism, type Ones are advised to avoid career choices that may involve a lot of criticism. It's also not a good idea to go for a job that you don't feel makes a difference. When in the wrong work environment, people will consider you non-adaptable, too demanding, and unrealistic. Be mindful of what your personality requires and the fact that you care about doing work that matters and being recognized for your dedication and commitment as an idealist. While I cannot tell you what your ideal job is, I can encourage you to avoid roles like Customer Service, Auditor, and Management assistant. Such career roles will not align with your strengths and only expose the aspects of you that need healing.

Type One Wing 2 - The Activist

The second Wing influences type One in subtle but significant ways. In this Wing, the emphasis is on service and developing deep relationships. Does that sound like you? Here are some more qualities:

- Sensitive to the needs of the people around you.
- Genuine love for humanity.
- Interested in mentoring opportunities and building one-to-one relationships.
- Always standing for what's right.

The main underlying qualities remain the same, but there will be some changes in the expression of a 1w2. Let's observe the differences between the two.

Healthy 1w9 personalities tend to view the world both imaginatively (as ideal as they wish it to be) and they also consider all the facts to keep themselves grounded. They try their best to maintain peace wherever they are. As a healthy 1w9, these individuals do a better job overcoming some of their shortcomings, e.g., when they make a mistake because they value maintaining that sense of peace. But at the end of the day, they still repress their emotions. This quality stems from the influence of their Nine Wing.

On the other hand, healthy 1w2 are more in tune with their emotions and allow themselves to feel anger, sadness, etc. The 1w2 personality is also more compassionate and helpful, more so with those they have close relationships. For a 1w2, it's not just about doing what's right for the greater good and making a difference in the world; it's also about developing real and deep connections.

Unhealthy 1w9 personalities tend to struggle with severe self-criticism and detachment, especially from their surroundings. Disassociating themselves is one of their coping mechanisms. On the other hand, unhealthy 1w2 personalities tend to become highly bossy. Instead of detaching and closing themselves off, they feel the need to take charge of every situation because they believe they know what's right. They might drown in self-pity in their low periods and whine about how mistreated they are. Unlike unhealthy 1w9, these individuals are incredibly vocal about their disappointment and disapproval of others, including their loved ones, which can make them quite unbearing. Unhealthy 1w2 personalities likely grow into these types of adults because, during their childhood, they received unfair treatment from their parents. As children, the 1w2 felt alone and isolated, especially if they got abused by the same person who was meant to protect them. However, any type One can unlearn their unhealthy emotional patterns and way of thinking. When a 1w2 moves in the direction of growth and heals those old wounds, they transform into compassionate, logical, and caring individuals that people love to be around.

In the workplace, type 1w2 personality loves to be in a leadership position where they can organize and manage people. As a 1w2, some of the best careers you can get into include:

- Nursing
- Law
- Real Estate
- Religious Worker
- Social Worker
- Medicine
- Politics

Again, be mindful of the career or job role you choose because some roles may cause you to feel unappreciated, or it may cut you off from direct day-to-day contact with people you can serve. Accounting, Retail representatives are just a few examples of roles that might not be a good fit for your overall personality and your wing type.

The path from anger to serenity begins when you become aware of your anger and how it drives you and causes suffering. As a classic Type One, you may not necessarily be aware of the under-lying anger that manifests are irritation and frustration, but it's time to become aware. You've learned that it's not okay to express your anger directly. So, much of it is hiding in your body. What's needed is for you to move into the healing zone and find your Serenity. In the Enneagram language, serenity is the Virtue of type 1.

If you're a One, then when at your best, you exhibit these strengths:

You're diligent, responsible, reliable, conscientious, and have a high degree of self-discipline. You're very sincere and have a strong sense of idealism.

When your strengths get out of balance or are used in unhealthy ways, they lead to:

Rigidity. Becoming too critical of yourself and others for not living up to your high standards. You also become controlling and moralistic. You might push yourself too hard, becoming obsessed with details and getting things done to perfection. Unfortunately, that also causes you to neglect yourself and cut out rest and relaxation.

SUBTYPES FOR TYPE ONE

An Enneagram subtype (also known as an instinctual subtype or instinctual variant) combines your main Enneagram type One and your survival instinct. There are three survival instincts that we can default to, and although all three are present in each of us, we tend to activate one at any given time. The other two remain neutral and under-developed, respectively. That is, you'll be overly aware of the first subtype (dominant), the second will be neutral (secondary), and the third won't even feel like it's part of you because it's totally underdeveloped, making it your blind spot(tertiary).

So when you read all three types, notice which one feels strongly connected to how you show up and which one you feel zero connection to. That will give you an idea of how your variants are stacked up in order of priority and influence.

Self-Preservation One (SP)

The Pioneer is the self-preservation instinct for a type One and is driven mainly by the need to tend to physical needs and anxiety. An SP 1 needs to conquer their environment and achieve order. We would term this subtype the more stereotypical perfectionist because they care a lot about being right and correct all the time. The main focus is also on being orderly and organized with their health, finances, home, and family matters. SP 1s engage in material achievements to overcome those feelings of worry and anxiety over security and survival. Despite the incessant worry, SP 1 knows how to "keep it together" and often comes across as warmer and friendlier than the other subtypes.

It's easy for an SP 1 to mistype as a type Six. SP 1s tend to suppress their anger even more than their other two subtypes. A common theme here would be the thought, "I need to be good and honorable with my family and meet my physical needs."

Does this sound more like you? Don't worry if it doesn't. Keep reading to identify your most dominant variant.

Social One (SO)

The Social Reformer is the Social One subtype and is driven mainly by the need to belong and be accepted in their community or group. All Type Ones are social and pro-change and reformation, but this particular subtype is more invested in social justice and fairness. They work extra hard to be role models and show others the right way to live. Although the SO 1s also repress anger, they are more okay with showing it.

It's easy to mistype an SO 1 as a type Three or type Five. Unfortunately, they can also be non-adaptable in their quest to uphold society's highest morals and standards. A common theme here would be the thought, "I need to be good and honorable with my community who depend on me."

Does this sound more like you? Don't worry if it doesn't. Just keep reading to identify your most dominant variant.

One-to-One/ Sexual One (SX)

The Evangelist is the one-to-one instinct for a type One, and they are mainly driven by the need to be right and perfect with their intimate connections. Please note that SX instinct refers to both platonic and romantic relationships. SX 1s are the countertype of Type One, which means they don't react to their dark side as a typical One would. Instead of repressing their anger and working hard to achieve self-perfection, they project it outward and focus on perfecting others. SX 1s struggle with zealousness and jealousy if you dig deeper. On the surface, they may still show a lot of self-control but hang around them long enough, and they will leak judgment and envy. Unlike the other subtypes, SX 1s will show their anger and resentment. It's easy to mistype an SX 1 for a type Eight. A common theme here would be the thought, "I need to be good and honorable with my intimate relationships."

Does that sound more like you? If not, that's okay. Keep exploring the rest of the book and become aware of which descriptions resonate most with you. Sometimes it takes a little more digging to uncover your type. If you've already identified as a Type One, you'll love the next chapter on tips for growth and improvement.

CHAPTER 6

WORK AND LIFESTYLE TIPS FOR TYPE 1S

Before we can talk about the positive changes you can make in your life, it's essential to address some of the ways you've been unconsciously holding yourself back and the struggles you're likely to face on this quest for self-improvement. Don't worry, most of this chapter is dedicated to what you can do to make things better in your world, but as I like to say, before shooting an arrow in any direction, be clear on the target.

Every Type One has a few blind spots, and by now, it shouldn't come as a surprise that most of them tend to be impulsive and natural. Anger is the first, and I'm sure, as a Type One, you know this all too well. You may not realize that despite your best attempts to hide your unresolved emotions, they still leak out in the form of body posture, facial expressions, tone, and other body language cues. For a present and observant person, they will feel and read your energy no matter calm you try to be. The anger you tend to experience usually comes from the high standards and expectations you have in your mind, which, unfortunately, few people in the world can live up to. Another way people can tell you have unresolved issues is through your over-criticism. While you do it with good intentions, very few people like to be criticized or judged. I think even you don't enjoy criticizing yourself, right? That's why many consider over criticism to be a negative trait. Let's find a better approach where you can still reform and improve your environment without going overboard in criticism and judgment. The last blindspot I want to make you aware of is the tendency to be too rigid. That tends to come from repressed feelings. If you tend to view emotions as a waste of time and productivity, you're likely repressing yourself and other people's emotions in your interactions. It's a wonderful trait to approach situations rationally and separate emotions from facts, especially when solving a problem, so let's aim to create a balance here. Repressed emotions never end well, and your life and relationships will improve when you learn to process emotions at the appropriate time, of course. What are some other struggles you may encounter on this quest of self-discovery? Let's identify the top ones.

STRUGGLES OF ENNEAGRAM ONE

Setting unrealistic expectations

The urgent need to always be honest, responsible, ethical, and hardworking can lead to unrealistic expectations of yourself. You set such high standards, which is excellent, but that can sometimes become your Achilles heel. Most people appreciate your integrity and would be okay with you even if you only hit 99% of your intended goals. Still, I know with you, nothing is good unless it's 100% right. So you might be in the habit of berating and being too hard on yourself. The lower you are on the development scale, this need to be perfect turns into a dark, twisted personality that's totally unhealthy for you and those around you.

What to do: If you recognize the tendency to push, punish or criticize yourself too much, it's time to learn some self-acceptance practices. The more you grow towards self-acceptance, the less demanding that inner critic will be and the easier it will be to accept others.

Never good enough

The classic "I'm never good enough" pain on your side is actually a common experience for all Type Ones. Flaws, mistakes, and defects seem more overwhelming for a Type One than any other Enneagram. Unfortunately, living in this energy of not being good enough is extremely draining and terrible for your health.

What to do: The feeling of not being good enough is mainly between the unhealthy and average levels of development. It comes from a lack of self-forgiveness. Take a moment now and observe how you've been extra strict and unforgiving to yourself. Choose to change that for the better.

Corruption and bad people overwhelm you

Our world can be a bit much for an idealistic and goal-oriented individual who lives with integrity. There's so much corruption going on, and a lot of bad goes unpunished. I know it's a lot to take in and impossible to accept. Your desire for ethical integrity for yourself and others is truly noble. As long as you serve to make the world a better place in healthy ways that bring out the highest version of yourself, then, by all means, fight on. However, if you're at average or unhealthy levels of development where you strive to overcome moral adversity at the cost of sacrificing your own needs, we need to take a step back. The desire to promote higher values is a good one to pursue, but you can't do it from a place of remorse, pain, anger, and resentment where you think others are beneath you. That kind of superficial righteousness only turns you into a hypocrite. It makes you cynical, pessimistic, and negative. Nothing good ever comes from those emotional states.

What to do: If you find yourself being sarcastic, cynical, or condescending about the world and the people around you who aren't living up to your standards, it's time to switch gears. Develop a more open mindset and a positive attitude. Find the good that exists instead of only feeding yourself the bad you hate. And yes, that might include cutting out all your news, gossip, and social media consumption or at least minimizing it to a point. At the same time, increase time spent on positive and joyful activities and experiences. Find stories of empathy and great human accomplishments.

Taking things too seriously

One more struggle you'll need to tackle is that of taking yourself a bit too seriously. Are you rigid with your routine, emotions, relationships, and how others should behave around you to the point that it's off-putting? Perhaps for you, it's normal, but I bet those in your life might have a different experience. Let me be clear here, no one is attacking that relentless hardworking, no B.S quality that you have because it does serve a great purpose. We are simply encouraging you to find a healthy balance so you can also relax and enjoy some spontaneity and the "unknown" once in a while. By doing so, you can avoid becoming too rigid in life and creating mountains of tension mentally and physically. Have you ever felt like you were a bubbling pot of boiling water simmering with passion and rage yet too afraid to allow those emotions to come up so you could deal with them once and for all?

For most ones, letting the lid off their emotions is unacceptable. They believe in concealing their feelings and never allowing themselves to reveal anything but total composure. That makes having an intimate and open relationship with a Type One really challenging.

What to do: If you realize you're too rigid with your life, relationships, emotions, and any other area of yourself give yourself permission to just open up to someone you trust and share your plight. Allow yourself to break some eggs and let out that anger or just scream at the top of your voice. I know this will be hard to do, especially at those average and unhealthy levels of development. But awareness is the first step to transformation. Just recognizing some of your inner struggles and allowing yourself to face them instead of denying them is already progress. Now keep going.

OPPORTUNITIES FOR GROWTH PROFESSIONALLY

Let's uncover some of how you can start growing personally and professionally now that you're doing the inner work of moving up in your development.

- Embrace your inner child once again and find your playful side. We all have a curious childlike quality in us. Find yours. Start small with something as simple as playing with a dog at the park, joining Zumba class, or painting again. Did you enjoy baking as a child? Why not join a beginner's cooking class. When was the last time you laughed so hard until a bit of pee came out? Fill your Netflix and Hulu playlist with classics that make you laugh until your ribs hurt.
- Embrace and process all your emotions, especially your anger. Anger or any other emotion isn't inherently wrong to feel. It's when we dwell and make that our dominant state that things go awry. You are not a bad person because you get emotional or feel negative emotions.

Pretending emotions aren't really only increases your tension and internal stress. The body will break down when negative emotions are suppressed. That creates room for passive-aggressive behavior, leaky negative emotions, and diseases. It's time to learn healthy ways to process all feelings. We'll discuss some healthy habits that can enable you to process emotions at the end of this chapter.

- Learn to ask for help. I know this will sound crazy at first but asking for help from others makes you a stronger, better, and at times a more responsible person. It's what leaders know. Being open about what you need help with doesn't make you weak. It enriches your relationships and ensures you don't burn out in the process of achieving greatness. And when you do receive help, allow the person to help and approach the situation in their own way. Let go of the need to micro-control others to do things your way all the time. This is especially important in your professional life while dealing with colleagues.

- Silence that inner critic and retrain your self-talk. Retrain your mind to dwell on positive self-talk and become the cheerleader in your life. Your invitation now is to start speaking to yourself as you would a lover or your child. Be the parent or coach you never had growing up. Approach yourself with the greatest sensitivity and compassion, knowing that no one else can be good to you unless you are good to yourself. That inner critic only replays an old record set by your caregivers during childhood. It's been playing for so long that your brain thinks that's the norm. It's time to teach yourself some new tricks. Things like how to love yourself more, forgive yourself when things go wrong, and effectively communicate with yourself for the best outcome. The relationship with Self is sacred; it is the most important relationship you will ever have in this lifetime. You and your inner voice have been in this game called life since birth, and you'll be together till your last breath. Doesn't it make sense to make the experience one of love instead of criticism?

ENNEAGRAM TYPE ONE UNDER STRESS

When Type One experiences stress, the first fallback is their unhealthy traits, including becoming critical, judgmental, and berating. If the stress and pressure persist, the One falls into the path of disintegration, as we discussed in arrows and their meaning, leading to the expression of some unhealthy traits of Type 4. That turns an average and unhealthy One into a moody, envious, withdrawn, melancholic and irritable person. But it doesn't have to be that way. Perfectionism is dialed up, and they struggle to accept any kind of flaw or mistake in themselves or others.

With this new awareness of how stress might lead you down a path of disintegration and further away from your true and highest version, here are a few healthier ways to deal with stress and pressure.

Schedule a day or chunks of hours to simply relax.

- While at work, take numerous planned breaks between activities to beat burnout and avoid getting too worked up about the problem.
- Invest time nurturing your inner child and being around fun-loving people (e.g., friends, siblings, etc.)
- Resist the urge to binge-watch or listen to sappy or angsty films and songs. That's just the unhealthy individualists (4) trying to take over the situation.

Instead, find something upbeat and humorous to watch and laugh at as much as possible.

RELATIONSHIPS

Both romantic and professional relationships must be honored when you're an Enneagram One. So it shouldn't be surprising that people consider you a loyal, reliable, and trustworthy person. They might feel like you can be too rigid or pushy, especially when things aren't getting done to the standards you set, but most people embrace the challenges of dating or working with your personality. Below are some tips to help you make things even better.

Be easy on yourself.

- Whenever you disagree with another, try to remember that neither of you is 100% right or wrong.
- Allow the other person (especially in a romantic relationship) to take the lead and do things their way without imposing your standards. It doesn't have to be all the time, but just periodically give them a chance.
- Sharing your feelings and expressing pleasant and unpleasant emotions is healthy when you're in an intimate relationship. Vulnerability can be a good thing.
- Allow yourself (sometimes) to just let go and be silly. This is especially important when you're dating. Relax and just enjoy the moment.
- While at work, let your co-workers understand you by clearly communicating your expectations, how you like to work, what you value, and how much you care about growth and improvement. The more your colleagues can

understand your point of view, the easier it will be for them to support you.

RELATIONSHIP TIPS WITH OTHER TYPES

Here's what you can expect and improve upon when you have a relationship with other Enneagram Types.

Type 1 & Type 1: With a fellow Type One, you're in that perfectly mirrored relationship where you get each other. You have high standards and strong convictions, and you want things done well. You both value integrity, honesty, and goodness. You're responsible, conscientious people who always act appropriately, and you enjoy the mutual respect and trust you've built. It's great to know you're with someone who has the same work ethic, thoughtfulness, and moral code you have.

A challenge you might face in this relationship is that you can become overly critical of each other because you're so similar. When your strong convictions land on different sides, you can become indignant. And when you do have a firm agreement, you may become too judgmental of those that don't see things your way because you believe it's the only "right" way. Another issue is that you both repress anger, especially when operating at average or lower levels of development, and typically those emotions leak out as resentment toward the other. Grow together by developing as a couple to higher levels of expression. Realize that you don't need to fuss over the little details of how the other isn't measuring up. Also, create time for fun and something that enables you to be silly together. A weekend getaway, summer vacation, or a night out can help you keep that fun aspect alive. And when you disagree on opinions, remember to soften your perspectives and allow the other the safety and freedom to have their different point of view even if you don't agree with it.

Type 1 & Type 2: With Type Two, you're in a warm, nurturing relationship. You're both doers who care about serving others and making the world better. Your partner brings grace and softness that's beneficial to your more rigid personality. You're good at taking care of the practical things in life and paying detailed attention to things which makes the Two feel valued. You're both present with each other, enjoy completing tasks, and working together toward a shared purpose.

A challenge you might face is during the conflict. You believe staying rational is the best way to move forward, and your partner tends to be more emotional. Another issue might arise due to the Two's desire for a more profound emotional connection, which might feel overwhelming to you, creating some distance. Grow together by openly communicating what you both need in the relationship. Be more intentional and descriptive to avoid misunderstanding. Carve out time to nurture and discuss your relationship without discussing other projects.

Type 1 & Type 3: With Type Three, the relationship is dynamic and task-oriented, and you enjoy accomplishing things together. You admire the Three's can-do attitude and ability to get things done, while your partner appreciates your sense of responsibility and unwavering commitment. You support each other's endeavors, and when conflict arises, you both believe that staying rational is the best way to figure things out.

A challenge you might face with this relationship is getting so consumed by your projects and talks that date nights can feel like a business meeting. In other words, you may not really be nurturing the relationship itself even when you're spending time together. Another issue is that Threes are shapeshifters, which might make you feel like your partner is manipulative or shallow. On the other hand, your partner might feel like you're too rigid or stifling, and your perfectionism may not be well received, especially if you're giving critical feedback. Grow together by prioritizing rest time. Make time for your relationship outside of projects and tasks. Keep an open communication at all times and avoid letting disagreements get out of hand.

Type 1 & Type 4: With a Four, you can cultivate a deep, meaningful relationship. You're both idealists with a vision of how the world could be. You help the Four create boundaries in their life and get a bit more structured, and they help you loosen up a bit and think outside the box. While you are opposites in many ways, your energies complement each other well, especially when operating under healthy levels of development.

A challenge you might face in this relationship is the negative impact of internalizing criticism. You can easily get overwhelmed by the Four's emotions and become resentful. On the other hand, the Four can lash out at your critique and constant correction even though you might just be trying to help them become better. Grow together by embracing your different approaches to life. Emphasize the things you have in common and find value in the things that make you different.

Type 1 & Type 5: With a Five, you're in a stable, dependable relationship with someone who pays attention to details almost as much as you. You and your partner are quick to observe things that others typically miss. You're thoughtful, hard-working, and understand each other well. The Five brings thoughtfulness, curiosity, competence, and depth to the relationship. Your high standards and steadiness are desirable to the Five. You enjoy being independent and structured boundaries in your relationship because it means you never overwhelm each other.

A challenge you might encounter in your relationship is when you have a difference in opinion. You believe in objectivity, so there's no changing your mind once you find the truth. On the other hand, Fives are open to evolving all their ideas as they learn more information. This difference can create frustration as your partner perceives you as too rigid while you might feel like they are not predictable. Another issue that might arise is that your advice may feel more like criticism for a Five who is very sensitive to criticism, which may cause them to withdraw and turn silent. This silence may cause you to feel insecure about your relationship. Grow together by openly communicating and learning to hold each other's ideas as valid even when you're not in agreement. Affirm each other and remind one another that you are there for each other.

Type 1 & Type 6: With a Six, you're in a committed, responsible, secure relationship. You both value duty and loyalty. The community matters to you, and you both want to make the world a better place. The Six is witty and help you lighten up, and you help your partner feel more grounded and safe. The relationship thrives because you feel like you can count on each other and make an effort to show each other love.

A challenge you might face in this relationship is during conflicts because you tend to become critical and resentful, making the already anxious Six insecure and fearful about the relationship. It turns the Six into a doubtful, skeptical person, which can frustrate you because they seem inconsistent and irrational when insecurity levels rise. Grow together by maintaining calm during conflicts. Try to keep a level head and encourage the Six to express how they feel without overreacting. You should regularly find little ways to be spontaneous together and add more fun into your life.

Type 1 & Type 7: With a Seven, the relationship is dynamic and adventurous, and there's a lot of spontaneity that takes you out of your comfort zone. In many ways, you're opposites, but when operating at healthy levels of development, the relationship thrives because you complement each other well. The Seven helps you celebrate life every day and find fun in all you do. You help ground the Seven and create a sense of stability and conscientiousness that they need.

A challenge you might experience is when the relationship hits a slump. Sevens get bored super fast and tend to feel trapped when they have to be in a predictable routine which is your thing. You might feel like you're in a relationship with a child who doesn't want to grow up, and your partner may feel like you're being a bully. At average and unhealthy levels, Sevens don't know how to handle slumps or obstacles, so they tend to run away from any kind of conflict or unpleasantness. While you're trying to be rational and work things out, they might be completely unwilling to work through problems. Invest time learning how to process unpleasant emotions together. Have those tough talks, and then reward yourselves for doing it. Appreciate the balance the other brings. Grow together by working on rising to higher levels of development.

Type 1 & Type 8: With an Eight, your relationship is truthful, dependable, and profound. You stand firm in your convictions, and both take responsibility for right the wrongs in the world around us. The Eight is intensely loyal and protective of you and the relationship, and you love that. You're trustworthy, detailed, systematic, fair, and truthful, and that's very attractive to an Eight. This can be a very intentional and deeply fulfilling relationship when cultivated correctly.

A challenge you might face is your differing energies and how you deal with tension or conflict. You prioritize self-control and choose your words carefully, but the Eight is more expressive and, at times, explosive with anger. Their directness may come across the wrong way, which can be highly frustrating for you. You both need to be in control, which often leads to a battle of wills during conflicts. Grow together by reminding each other that you're on the same team. Find activities like mindfulness practices that you enjoy doing together to help you be more present and calm.

Type 1 & Type 9: With a Nine, you're in a comfortable, stable, harmonious easy going relationship. Both of you are ethical, considerate, and self-sacrificing, and you're propelled by a deep sense of purpose. The Nine enables you to be more self-accepting and self-forgiving because they are always comforting and accepting. You help bring a sense of duty and work ethic to the Nine so they can create more of what they desire.

A challenge you might face in this relationship is how you deal with anger and conflict. Although you're both in the body triad, where is the emotional wound, you process it very differently. The Nine avoids it and tries to repress anger to keep the peace while you suppress it and do everything to be appropriate at all times. All this pent-up anger leaks from time to time, especially during tension. Stubbornness, resentment, and passive-aggressiveness are issues you'll need to overcome to keep your relationship healthy. Grow together by finding healthy ways to deal with conflict and clear the air. Affirm one another and the relationship whenever you're working through a conflict. Encourage your partner to voice their issue and let it go once resolved.

AFFIRMATIONS FOR ENNEAGRAM TYPE 1

Read through the following affirmations and find a handful that resonates to help you shift into a healthier version of yourself.

- I embrace and accept myself completely.

- I forgive myself easily and move on.
- I forgive others easily and move on.
- I accept who I am.
- I choose to focus on finding good in others and giving my attention to what's working.
- I choose to be kind and compassionate to those I work with.
- I accept that everyone is doing the best they can with their level of awareness.
- I choose to see mistakes as learning opportunities.
- I love and approve of myself.

Remember, affirmations only work when what you say and feel are in synch.

DAILY ROUTINES FOR GROWTH AND HAPPINESS

- Practice self-care daily. By making self-care a priority, you allow yourself to dissolve the critical aspects of your personality. You could list different self-care activities that you could do for each day of the week, including taking a bubble bath and treating yourself to a spa session or a massage. Get creative and really show yourself some love.
- To make sure the tendency for perfection isn't stressing you out, follow the path of integration and pick up healthy, fun habits that you enjoy. Do you love board games? Great. Why not play games over the weekend with a friend. What about dancing? Consider signing up for some dance classes or try cooking a new recipe.
- Practice mindfulness. Some people prefer to meditate or do some yoga as part of their mindfulness practice. Try

both and see which aligns with your lifestyle. If neither brings you to that present state of mindfulness, experiment with taking mindfulness walks or mindfulness showers. There is no right or wrong way to center yourself and become fully present. The only thing that matters is that you do it consistently.

- Keep investing in your personal and professional growth. Don't be afraid to stretch beyond your comfort zone and join educational activities that aren't necessarily related to your work. The more range you can give yourself, the more you'll expand your awareness and perspective. An ever-expanding perspective is a key to development for a Type One.

- Make time to process your emotions. Nothing will change your life experiences more than choosing to face and process all your feelings boldly. You can schedule weekly emotions time where you step back and meet with all the emotions you had to check during the week. That enables you to have more control over your feelings rather than being controlled by them. It also eliminates the danger of falling into stress and disintegration.

CHAPTER 7

ENNEAGRAM TYPE 2

THE HELPER OR GIVER

T his chapter and the next will go in-depth on the Enneagram type Two, commonly referred to as the helper or giver. The title - helper is a perfect fit for this enneatype because these individuals thrive when taking care of and nurturing others. Type Twos are empathetic, warm-hearted, gentle, generous, caring, and naturally friendly. Their need to feel and be loved is predicated on how much others need and appreciate them. Helpers tend to be self-sacrificing to the point of self-neglect because they have such a strong belief that their value comes from helping others first. Enneagram Type Twos fall into the heart or Feeling Center making shame one of the main emotions that hinder personal growth and evolution, especially if unresolved. One of the great gifts of an Enneagram Type Two is their interpersonal skills. You'll find them at the center of action either at work or in a family set-up doing everything they can to ensure all parties have what they need. That can be everything from lending a hand on a project, offering a shoulder to cry on, or babysitting your child so you can have an hour to rest. There's no task too big for a Two to say yes to, and sometimes, this can back-fire on them, creating a lot of inner turmoil.

Although Twos are always gentle, positive, and caring towards others, they have a dark side that sometimes leaks out in temperamental outbursts, especially when they feel underappreciated. Most people get surprised that Twos can get angry, and indeed this doesn't happen very often. Still, it's good to realize that even the gentle Two can be pushed to their point of emotional eruption. Do you recognize any of these signs in yourself? If you've already done an Enneagram Test that typed you as a Two, continue reading to learn more about some unconscious patterns you may not have recognized. I like to combine self-study and the Enneagram Test because it enables me to concentrate more on my enneatype and uncover more of myself without wasting time. But even if you didn't take the test, you might still type yourself accurately if you read each chapter in the book and reflect honestly. With the information you learn here, begin to notice your patterns and incorporate the suggestions and recommendations given in the next chapter so that you can stop self-neglecting.

As a Type Two, your greatest desire is to see others happy, and that's a great intention. We just need to make sure achieving that goal doesn't come at the cost of your well-being and personal evolution.

Many Twos who aren't yet operating at higher and healthier levels of development often fall into self-neglect and people-pleasing habits. It's a slippery slope when sacrificing one's need to help others. The end result is typically emotions of resentment, anger, frustration, and disappointment. That's especially the case when Twos don't receive the rewards or the credit they feel they deserve for all their efforts.

STRENGTHS OF A TWO

Twos have a natural ability to recognize the needs of others. They play a strong supporting and encouraging role for those around them.

Twos have tremendous empathy, especially for the lonely, marginalized, and undervalued people around them. They always act from a place of generosity and love. Nothing is too much of an ask for a Two, which is why people love being around them.

Type Twos know how to build welcoming homes for themselves and others.

Key personality traits of Type Two

- Warm, approachable, and kind.
- Excellent team player.
- Gentle and caring.

Common hobbies for a Type Two

- Cooking
- Gardening
- Volunteering
- Socializing

FEARS AND WEAKNESSES

By now, you have enough clarity about a Type Two's need to be and feel loved and how that's tied into their self-worth. Love is one of the highest and most important human needs that we all have. For Type Two, having that sense of being loved by others is core to their identity and happiness.

At times this push to receive love because they give it to others first is actually rooted in fear.

What's the Basic Fear driving this behavior? The fear of being unworthy of receiving unconditional love.

As a Type Two, you want to be needed by other people because that reassures you of your place in their lives and affections. Much of this thinking comes from childhood experiences that we'll touch upon shortly. Still, we realize now that people pleasing and caring for others so you can receive love isn't a sustainable way of experiencing unconditional love. A fundamental weakness you must overcome is the continuous need to seek approval from others. That only perpetuates your self-doubt and causes further damage to your self-image.

Your sensitivity to other people's emotions and needs is a strength, but only if it doesn't override your own needs. I know that saying "No" is one of the hardest things you could ever do because nothing matters more than maintaining great relationships. Still, it's time you learned that sometimes being a good caregiver and nurturer requires one to say NO. And just so you know, that doesn't make you any less loveable or worthy of love.

Our goal is to move you higher in your development, into the healthy levels of expression where you can finally find the balance between helping others and fulfilling your needs and purpose.

Growing up in an environment where your basic emotional needs (especially unconditional love) were lacking means you had to adapt to other people's expectations and repress your own desires to survive. Perhaps somewhere during your upbringing, you may have picked up the message that you can only receive affection when you do something good for those who care for you. Now that you're past that stage in your life, it's time to heal some of these wounds and step into your true power.

How does this Basic Fear often manifest itself?

The conditioned belief that stating your needs is wrong has caused you to fear saying "NO" to anyone because you're afraid of rejection or losing love. So you keep saying yes even when it hurts. That dissolves all personal boundaries and likely leads to self-neglect.

You may also have difficulty dealing with tension, relationship conflicts, and disagreements. Many Twos share that whenever they get into an argument with a loved one, they can't focus on work or anything else until that situation is resolved. We also know that this topic of addressing needs is a bit tricky for a Type Two to face. If you're feeling all kinds of discomfort as you read this, that's okay. You're not alone. You might have been raised with the belief that your needs don't matter, and maybe you even feel ashamed that you have needs (I have a friend who once shared that she felt ashamed to ask her husband for anything). Some fears manifest in extreme ways where the individual becomes resentful because they recognize they have unmet needs. Still, they're too ashamed to boldly ask for what they need, and so they just hate on others. Some unconsciously become manipulative. They offer help and serve others purely because they want to get something in return. These are the people in the lower levels of development. As a Type Two, it's essential, to be honest with yourself, get clear on where you stand when it comes to meeting your needs, and then begin the work of moving through and out of that fear state. That's when you will finally stop living at the mercy of others and their approval and instead discover your true value and unconditional love.

DESIRES AND MOTIVATIONS

The Basic Desire for a Type Two is to be loved. With that desire comes the core motivation or the energy that pushes an individual forward in life. By understanding the motivations behind your Enneagram Type Two, you can better identify where you are meant to be in life or what purpose you would best serve. For Type Two, the desire to achieve a sense of belonging and be loved and needed by others is inherent in their thoughts and actions. As a Two, you've seen how easy it is for you to step into any situation and immediately identify what other is feeling and what they need. You're the person that's always there to cheer others on and support them on their journey. It takes keen attentiveness and care to respond to other people's needs. True to your personality, your purpose is closely tied to nurturing and building relationships. Being the friend everyone would love to have, you have a lot to give. So as you begin your journey of self-healing and growth, don't discard these qualities that make you exceptional. Instead, find healthy ways to integrate them into your life in healthy ways that promote unconditional love. Notice how important love is in your life. In fact, as we break down your core values, you'll realize that becoming more of yourself doesn't cancel out your relationships. It only enables you to serve and care for others from a place of overfill rather than dependency and lack. Let's name some of the top values your personality identifies with most.

Core values

- Love
- Family and friendship
- Kindness and empathy
- Altruism, selflessness
- Compassion

- Serving others
- Thoughtfulness
- Appreciation
- Generosity

Type Two celebrities and famous people you might know include Singer Dolly Parton, Mathematician and Writer Lewis Carrol, Singer and music producer Stevie Wonder, Actress and First lady of the United States Nancy Reagan, Catholic nun and missionary leader Mother Teresa, Television host Mr. Rogers and Actress Debbie Reynolds.

Wondering if you could be a Type Two? Here are some personality indicators:

1. You value relationships above all else. Nothing is more important to you than family, friends, and even acquaintances.
2. Offering support, helping, and serving others is something you genuinely enjoy.
3. You're drawn to careers that are service-oriented and people-facing.
4. You feel deeply hurt when people don't reciprocate your generosity and helpfulness.
5. You're sensitive to criticism
6. You have an innate ability to know what people are seeking in a friend and always seem to know exactly what to say and do
7. One of the things you struggle with is the concept of selfishness. You do not want to ever come across as selfish, but you also don't like it in others.
8. You tend to overcommit and struggle with setting clear boundaries.

9. Having a warm, inviting home is extremely important to you.
10. You sometimes worry that you're worthless unless you give to others or help them somehow.
11. At your best, you feel creative, authentic, comfortable with who you are, and very much enjoy creative expression.

YOUR WINGS

Wings are the numbers that you find directly adjacent to your Enneagram Type. As a Type Two, you have -

- The Enneagram Two with One-Wing
- The Enneagram Two with Three-Wing

While many believe both wings are active in each of us, one Wing tends to be more dominant and influential in our lives. Studying the arrows and their meaning can enable you to figure out which Wing is influencing your behavior and thought patterns at any given stage of life.

Meaning of your Wing

If you're a *2w1 (Two with One-Wing)*, then you're more concerned about supporting others and being seen as a responsible figure. With this Wing, your morals play an important role in behaving and relating to others. You're willing to do anything for a friend or loved one as long as it matches your morals. Unfortunately, you also tend to be too critical of yourself, as is common to an enneatype One. You have lots of trouble openly expressing your needs.

If you're a *2w3 (Two with Three-Wing)*, you're more ambitious than the 2w1 and way more extraverted. You also make an excellent leader because you have a bit of that competitive and winner's mindset that's influenced by the enneatype Three.

The Arrows and what they mean

Looking closely at the Enneagram symbol, we can see the connecting lines and arrows for your type, giving us further insight into how you react to stress and challenges and what opportunities for growth you have at any given point. Thus, moving toward disintegration or unhealthy stress (8), you would be overly needy, aggressive, and even a little dominating at Eight. However, moving toward growth and integration (4), you transform that prideful quality and become more self-nurturing and emotionally aware like a healthy Four. Although you can move in the direction of disintegration or integration at any point in your life, the primary influencer of your behavior and what you express is determined by your current level of development. Let's see if you can spot where you are so you can start moving upward to the highest version of yourself.

LEVELS OF DEVELOPMENT

Levels of Development arise from Riso and Hudson's teachings and the founders of the Enneagram Institute, which is a great place to take your Enneagram Test. Their theory posits that all individuals fall into one of nine levels of functioning. The lowest level is nine, and the highest is level one. The levels are divided into a triad that subcategorizes these levels as healthy (1,2,3), average levels (4,5,6), and unhealthy levels (7,8,9).

Unhealthy Levels

Level 9: This is the lowest and most destructive state for a Type Two to be at unless they are still in infancy. As adults, if a person is still trapped here, they feel victimized, abused, and powerless. They can excuse and rationalize their actions no matter how horrible because they are resentful and angry at the world and others. Twos at this stage struggle with a lot of health problems as they vindicate themselves by "falling apart" and burdening others.

Level 8: At this level, an unhealthy Type Two is very prideful and entitled. They are domineering, aggressive, and coercive. This individual chooses to use manipulation to get what they want from others. Nothing they give comes from a place of generosity because they always expect something back.

Level 7: This is the least dangerous unhealthy level for a Two. A Type Two at this level is highly deceptive and selfish in their behavior. Although they can be manipulative and self-serving, they're not extreme or overly aggressive. Instead, they will use guilt to get what they want, belittle and undermine others, and abuse things like food and medication to get sympathy.

Average Levels

Level 6: A Type Two at this level is overbearing, condescending, presumptuous, and walks with an air of self-righteousness for all the good they do. This Two tends to overrate just how much good they are doing and feel indispensable (as though people owe them). Although their efforts are directed toward others, it is done to garner praise, love, and affection.

Level 5: At this level of development, Type Two expresses their neediness by becoming too possessive, co-dependent, and intrusive. This Type Two wants others to depend on them, but at the same time, they expect something in return. They simply overdo their acts of kindness to the point of meddling and control, all in the name of love.

Level 4: This average Type Two craves a connection with others and struggles the most with people pleasing. They are overly friendly, emotionally demonstrative, and full of "good intentions" about everything. Showing and receiving love is of supreme importance for this Two. They will wear themselves out trying to get approval and do things for others that demonstrate how loving they can be.

Healthy Levels

Level 3: At this level, we begin to see real growth and transformation as this Type Two expresses a more nurturing, generous, and genuinely loving aspect of their nature. This individual is awakening, encouraging and appreciative. They can see good in others, and although serving others is still super important, they also tend to their own needs. That makes them pretty stable and genuinely kind in their acts.

Level 2: At this level of development, the total transformation has occurred for a Type Two, and we see the rise of a more empathetic, compassionate individual. This Two knows how to set clear boundaries and tend to their own needs and wants. They do not depend on the affection or approval of anyone but instead give from a place of fullness. This Type Two is warm-hearted, forgiving, sincere, thoughtful, and wonderful to be around.

Level 1: This is the holy grail for a Type Two. It's where the individual transcends and becomes their highest and most spiritually mature version. This Two knows how to love themselves and others. They are altruistic, humble, unselfish, and filled with unconditional love that radiates wherever they go.

TYPE TWO'S PASSIONS

Your dominant Passion as a Type Two is Pride. Pride in this context refers to the inability or unwillingness to acknowledge one's own suffering (something all Twos are very guilty of). The Passions (also known as the Deadly Sins) are our teachers. Most of us were taught to hide, avoid, and run away from the aspects that aren't pleasant. But here, we are encouraged to boldly face the parts of us that need healing so we can dissolve and transform a negative into a positive. You can also think of this Passion as vainglory because it's essentially pride in one's virtue. As a Two, helping others even at the cost of your own well-being and to the point of self-neglect is something you take great pride in. Yet, there is a deep lack in all that "giving" because it violates your wholeness. By following the thread presented by your Passion, you become aware of where you are relative to your highest Self and essential nature.

Pause for a moment and think about how often you feel the injustice or "unfairness" of others when you feel like the other didn't appreciate you or reciprocate enough. Wasn't it coming from a sense of entitlement and pride? As though they "owed" you for what you did for them? If you can become more aware of your Passion of Pride, you'll likely see that it's rooted in this sense of feeling unloveable or unworthy of receiving love. So you end up giving and ensuring others need you to guarantee that they will approve of and love you. Increasing your awareness of this opens up a new choice. It enables you to transform and start moving toward your Essence, which returns you back to your virtue of Humility.

CHILDHOOD AND EMOTIONAL PATTERNS OF TYPE TWO

Enneagram Type Twos are part of the Feeling or Heart Center of Intelligence, where shame is a dominant emotion that needs healing. The deadly sin for a Two is pride, but pride comes in various flavors. It's not just a matter of entitlement. It can also be an air of self-righteousness and need to be praised and outwardly appreciated for your strong support and good work. The worldview that to gain love and approval, you need to give to others and be needed by them causes you to attach your sense of value to this external validation. And while being a generous, supportive and attentive partner, friend, colleague, boss, or parent is an excellent thing, if you're doing it from a place of lack and disconnect, its expression may not be healthy. You might end up neglecting yourself and becoming too needy and co-dependent. What's needed for growth is humility so you can free yourself from the need to give to others to feel loved and valued. It's about realizing that you are whole, worthy of love, and complete just as you are. The path from pride to humility is the path of healthy integration and growth.

Type Two Wing 1- The Companion

A type Two with Wing One means the individual has all the qualities of a Two and a few of Enneagram One. Although you can be influenced by both Wings, the more dominant one will resonate deeply with you as your read these descriptions and learn how that shows up in behavior. Studying your primary personality and identifying your wing type will give you more insight into your behavior, childhood trauma, and how that's affecting your adult life. Type 2w1 comes across as optimistic and warm with high standards and expectations. Does that sound like you? Here are some more details of this personality:

- Caring
- Responsible
- Hardworking
- Empathetic
- Excellent listener
- Extremely likable and approachable
- Friendships and relationships are a bigger priority than anything else, even your own needs

Unfortunately, they struggle to live up to their own expectations. That perfectionism tends to be a constant source of anguish. They try hard to ensure they don't disappoint anyone because they fear rejection and failure as that would prove their hidden belief of not being good enough. The Companion puts everyone else's needs ahead of their own to cope with their fears and mitigate the constant worry of being alone. This constant need to do things for others turns a 2w1 into a total pushover at extreme levels.

The behavior may be rooted in a very strict childhood where parents or caregivers demanded a lot from this type. Often we find the 2w1 was given loads of responsibility at a really young age which made them learn to take on other people's problems and to feel guilty when things go wrong. It also made them associate receiving love and approval with giving to others first.

Type Two Wing 3- The Host

The Host is the charming and eloquent variation of the Ennea-gram Two. That might be one of the reasons they tend to be super popular in their social group and at work. Unlike the more worri-some and fearful 2w1, this type Two is bold, ambitious, and fear-less. Despite this boldness, 2w3 still has a strong need to be loved and needed by others. Hence, they tend to be more extravagant and outgoing than the 2w1 variation of their type. They are also more driven to take up leadership roles and might go as far as being a little rebellious to stand out from the crowd and prove themselves. 2w3 can be less emotionally sensitive. Despite the many similarities these two Wing types will have, the 2w3 experiences less personal distress than the 2w1. On the one hand, that increases traits like:

- Confidence
- Boldness
- Decisiveness

The natural ability in type Two to build deep relationships is expressed in healthy ways when a 2w3 is on the Path of Integration which causes others to trust and follow them naturally. On the other hand, it makes them more arrogant, pretentious, insensitive, and obsessive, especially at the lower levels of development. At their best, however, 2w3s are more self-aware and self-assured. They know how to support others even as they pursue their own ambitions. They develop a greater sense of balance between work and play.

If you're a Type Two, then at your best, you express these strengths:

You're generous, helpful, and love to provide support, guidance, and advice to others. You're a romantic at heart and easily maintain lasting relational connections. Tuning in to people's needs and feelings comes naturally to you. You always know what others need. You're energetic, engaging, enthusiastic, and great at getting things done.

When you move toward the unhealthy aspects of your personality, you exhibit these characteristics:

- You feel unlovable and unworthy if you're not giving to others. When you don't feel needed, you experience deep worry and fear that you're no longer valuable or loved. You're prone to a lot of self-shaming, self-judgment, and comparing yourself to others. Sometimes it oscillates between self-loathing and feeling superior to others. You get resentful and angry when you feel like your giving isn't reciprocated. You're prone to chronic self-neglect. You exhaust yourself by giving too much and investing too much in relationships.
- You're caring, energetic, loved by all, and quite popular in the workplace because people enjoy working with you. Your ability to uplift anyone and everyone is admirable. When operating from a healthy level of development, you easily convert negative energy into positive. Classic Type Twos have high emotional intelligence and always work productively and efficiently.

Best and worst careers for Type Twos

For any Type Two, a career that involves teamwork and supporting others is highly recommended. Choose a career that fulfills your social needs and allows you to influence others directly because that's one of your strengths. Your desire for approval and reassurance will be satiated if you work with superiors and co-workers who aren't afraid to express their appreciation of you. An environment where high energy, collaboration, and joy are promoted. Some careers that may offer this experience include teaching, counseling, therapy, psychology, becoming a religious leader, social worker, non-profit worker, or even a doctor.

Careers to avoid include salesperson, stockbroker, acting, modeling, or any industries that are likely full of rejection, criticism, and high competition. Such jobs may not be as fulfilling for a classic Two.

SUBTYPES FOR TYPE TWO

Your primary Enneagram Type Two further combines with your natural instincts to create subtypes generally stacked in order of dominance.

There are three survival instincts that we can default to, and although all three are present in each of us, we tend to activate one at any given time. The other two remain neutral and under-developed, respectively. Hence you'll be overly aware of the first subtype (dominant), the second will be neutral (secondary), and the third won't even feel like it's part of you because it's totally underdeveloped, making it your blind spot(tertiary).

So when you read all three types, notice which one feels strongly connected to how you show up and which one you feel zero connection to. That will give you an idea of how your variants are stacked up in order of priority and influence.

The Self-Preservation Two (SP)

The main quality is Privilege. SO Twos express themselves as the "cute" and charming individuals with very childlike energy. This Two is the countertype of the group and tends to display behavior that causes them to be mistyped for a different Enneagram Type like a 6 or 7. This individual is shy, charming, and wants to be loved and cared for. However, they resist being dependent on others and tend to be a little more withdrawn in an attempt to self-protect. Self-preservation Twos are more self-indulgent and hedonistic, always searching for pleasurable experiences to distract themselves from feelings of self-abandonment and inner deprivation.

The Social Two (SO)

Ambition is the main quality for this subtype. The SO Two is more interested in utilizing their seductive power intellectually to influence and attract groups, communities, and broader systems. They like to stand out from the crowd and often seek leadership roles. Such individuals enjoy being in the know and building their connections and competence. Less childlike than the other subtypes, it's easy to mistype this SO Two for an Eight or Three.

The One-to-One/ Sexual Two (SX)

Seduction is the main quality of this variant. This Type Two is more focused on their talent, seductive abilities, and using their energy to attract and build strong relationships. They care more about close connections on a 1-1 basis, whether that's a romantic or platonic setting. This Two can express personal needs a little better in an intimate setting. SX Twos are passionate, flexible, strong-willed, and even a little wild at heart, sometimes leading to a mistype with a 4.

CHAPTER 8
WORK AND LIFESTYLE TIPS FOR TYPE 2S

Before we discuss how you can improve yourself on this quest of self-discovery, we must explore some of the struggles you may experience on your journey. For some of you, the struggles already dominate your life, and if that's the case, you'll find the suggestions offered pretty helpful.

STRUGGLES OF AN ENNEAGRAM TWO

Learning to say "NO."

Type Two's biggest struggle is learning to add NO into their vocabulary. By not learning to say no, you also create opportunities for unkind people to take advantage of your goodness. The core desire to be loved and feel worthy is so attached to helping and serving others. So when someone asks for something, it feels like a battle to just say you can't or won't help out. Unfortunately, when you don't learn to set clear and healthy boundaries for yourself, you wear yourself thin and overgiving at the cost of your personal well-being. As a Two, your self-esteem revolves around giving and being selfless, but you need to know the difference between generosity, where you give from an overflow, and selfish giving, where you give because you believe it will get you the love, affection, and assurance you need.

What to do: Learn to give generously from a place of overflow and unconditional love, not neediness. Those who genuinely love you will not change their attitude or your relationship simply because you said no to a request. And when a favor or demand is placed on you that goes against your values or jeopardizes your well-being, have the courage to say no.

Feeling unloved

If you grew up in an environment where you were taught that love comes at a price, you only felt loved when you did something for someone. This unresolved emotion will likely influence your adulthood. Average and unhealthy Type Twos will struggle with this feeling the most, and it often leads to all kinds of diseases. Pause for a moment and honestly think about how you feel. Do you constantly worry that people only love you for what you do and not for who you are as a human being?

What to do: Work on increasing your understanding of love. It's time to learn that people love you for who you are, not what you do.

Feeling misunderstood

Type Twos are naturally empathetic, highly attuned to other people's emotions, and perceptive. Being this sensitive and tactful, you tend to know what others need even before they admit or recognize it. And while it's great for those around you, it can also lead to a lot of neglect because most of the time, you pay more attention and even prioritize the needs you recognize in others. Over time, that causes you to communicate your needs even less.

I have a friend who was stuck in an unhappy relationship for five years because she couldn't find the right time to break up with her boyfriend. It sounds silly for the rest of us, but as a Type Two, you probably understand what it's like to live an empty and unseen life. If you've spent your life feeling like a dumping ground for other people's emotional baggage, it's time to put an end to that.

What to do: If you feel misunderstood or being taken advantage of, cultivate the courage to express your needs and emotions. Don't let resentment fester.

Grappling with the topic of selfishness

What qualifies as selfish in your world? That is a question you need to answer for yourself if you want real growth. It's okay to recognize that you have trouble taking care of yourself or giving yourself a break because you don't want to come across as selfish. Many Twos say they feel guilty when they get sick or can't help out a friend. That stirs up more feelings of unworthiness, and some even worry that people they love will abandon them if they ever act in selfish ways. No one can tell you what you should believe, but I do encourage you to rewrite your rules on what selfishness looks like for your own sake.

What to do: Assess your understanding of selfishness and make sure it allows you to take care of yourself and prioritize your needs.

OPPORTUNITIES FOR GROWTH

Let's uncover some of the ways you can start growing personally and professionally now that you're doing the inner work of moving to higher levels of development.

Prioritize your needs

The biggest growth area for you and the opportunity at hand is learning to tend to your needs first. If you don't, no one else will. Giving someone else the responsibility of keeping you happy and fulfilled gives away too much power and always results in disappointment and misunderstanding. The key to successful relationships, a sense of fulfillment, and increased self-worth is taking complete charge of your needs. So learn to take care of your mind, body, and spirit. Figure out what you need to lead a happy, balanced and healthy life. If you need assistance with resources or certain activities, ask for help but never hand over responsibility.

Assuming you did the inner work of determining what selfish is and isn't, start applying that in your daily engagements. For example, if while at work this week a colleague asks for you to help them complete a task over lunch hour, what should you do? Well, old, you would immediately say yes without giving it a thought. But now that you're growing and learning to become the best version of yourself, recall that your body needs nourishment. What impact will that have on your energy, focus, mood, and overall health by skipping lunch? Unless it's an emergency, the proper answer would be, "No, I'm sorry I can't help you during lunch, but I can try to find a different option if that works for you?"

This isn't an act of selfishness. It's common sense behavior from someone who has their priorities right.

Analyze your motives

Type Twos can be so selfless and giving for all the wrong reasons. I'm not here to judge but instead to expand your awareness so you can judge for yourself what your motives are at any given point. Do you frequently help someone because you expect them to reciprocate somehow? If so, that's a motive rooted in lack and selfishness that will not serve your sense of worthiness. It's easy for average and unhealthy Twos to become manipulative in their good deeds, so you always want to check in to ensure you are doing good because it feels good, not because you want something in return.

Tune into your real value

Most of the inner turmoil and struggles you experience with people will evaporate as you rise higher in your personal development. That's because the more you discover your true Self, the more you learn your true value. Soon enough, you stop being dependent on others to love you. If you do something good for someone, you don't do it for validation, affection, or to feel worthwhile. In fact, you only do it because you're overflowing with unconditional love. And whether the person acknowledges your efforts or not, it won't matter to you because your value and sense of worth are no longer attached to what others think of you but who you think you are. Can you feel the difference? This is such a powerful shift for a Two, and it will transform your life, so keep working at this. Keep walking this path of self-discovery until you know your value and who you really are.

ENNEAGRAM TYPE TWO UNDER STRESS

Type Twos dip into unhealthier versions of their traits, including pride, manipulation, and martyrdom, when under stress, either personal or professional. If the stress persists, they'll often move into the full-blown path of Disintegration we talked about earlier and pick up the average and unhealthy traits of Type 8. That includes becoming aggressive, pushy, controlling, demanding, argumentative, and tyrannical. As a Two, you may have noticed that you don't even feel or behave like yourself under certain stressful conditions. For instance, your usual caring, generous nature and deep desire to help others around you may get hijacked by some unknown dark force. You find yourself more harsh and blunt than usual. You probably become edgy and more aggressive, careless less about other people's feelings, and even lashing out when you feel invalidated. That often causes you pain and grief as you push away the people you care about or even avoid certain people in your life who need you just because you're trying to prove a point. This isn't true to your nature. So how can you beat stressful situations that trigger this dark side?

Things that typically stress a Two include:

- Being taken for granted
- Too much time alone
- Feeling left out
- Not getting affirmation or gratitude for their kind deeds
- Saying "yes" to too many things to the point of burnout.
- Not feeling needed

One of the most important things you can do for yourself when feeling stressed or irritated is to pause, step out of that stressful environment and just be with yourself for a little while.

Often the stress is triggered by taking on too many things all at once or focusing too much on others and neglecting yourself. When you can step away for an hour or a day and just tend to your own needs first, it usually brings back the sense of balance and harmony disrupted by stress.

Some of the activities you could indulge in to get you off that stress frequency include music therapy, painting, or some kind of artistic expression. You can even treat yourself by going for a massage, shopping, or booking a table for 1 at your favorite restaurant. Whatever uplifts you and centers your energy is a must if you want to process stress quickly and in a healthy way.

As you take time off to replenish your needs, remember to communicate with others. Let them know you're taking some alone time to heal, grow and nourish yourself and that you'll be back in communication at a specific time. That enables people to give you some space.

RELATIONSHIPS

Type Twos are naturally intuitive, empathetic, and caring in nature. So when it comes to friendships, professional team relationships, and companionships, Twos always excel.

You naturally make a wonderful parent, boss, team leader, and friend as a Two because of your supporting and compassionate nature. You're the person people come to when they feel hurt or troubled by something. People naturally open up, and your warmth is very soothing. At work, you'll always put others. First, your emotional intelligence is off the charts, so you know how to handle different personalities and facilitate healthy teamwork and collaboration. That enables you to be efficient, productive, and uplifting even in less-than-ideal situations. But you can only be this soothing warm light when you've grown to healthier levels of your own development.

RELATIONSHIP TIPS WITH OTHER TYPES

As a Two, you give yourself freely in any and all relationships because you desire to cultivate a fun, passionate, and happy partnership. Here are some ways to improve your relationships with other Enneagram Types.

Type 2 & Type 1: With a One, you're both doers who want to improve the world. You see the needs of others and act on them quickly. Type One is good at taking care of the practical things, and you as a Two offer softness and grace, which Ones typically struggle with. Since you have different approaches to emotional conflict, it can be overwhelming for Type One to understand your deep desire for connection. So grow together by finding time to be intentional about your relationship. Have an open dialogue that is strictly about your relationship and the balance between both your emotional needs.

Type 2 & Type 2: This is a match made in heaven with a fellow Two because you intuitively know what the other needs. You're generous and thoughtful toward each other, kind-hearted and affectionate. You constantly affirm each other, making you feel loved, valued, and seen. Be mindful about exhausting yourself and using up all your energy helping others, especially if it's starting to impact your relationship. Don't be afraid to admit that you both need help learning to tend to your individual needs. Never let pride or resentment get in the way of cultivating unconditional love in your relationship. Grow by learning to identify your own feelings and prioritize self-care.

Type 2 & Type 3: With a Three, you're a charming, passionate, engaging, and impactful power couple. You bring warmth, affirmation, and acceptance to the Three and that kind of love reminds the Type Three that they don't have to perform to be valuable. The Threes bring ambition, energy, and liveliness to your relationship, which inspires you to follow your dreams. Your confidence, attractiveness, and radiant energy make you a dynamic couple. The challenge comes in acknowledging and understanding your own feelings. Your helpfulness and desire for deeper emotional connection can get overwhelming for a Three. If you start feeling overlooked, taken for granted, or forgotten by your ambitious, task-oriented three, speak up. Grow together by learning how to have an open, intimate dialogue. Ask high-quality questions and engage with each other through reflective conversations to help you get in touch with your own feelings.

Type 2 & Type 4: With a Four, you're an intimate, deeply connected, and emotionally fulfilling couple. You see the Four's needs and offer friendly, supportive, understanding energy, while the Type Four brings creativity, humor, and honesty that you deeply enjoy. There are high expectations in this relationship, but you're not always good at communicating these expectations with each other. Because a Type Four is naturally reflective, they may not realize your needs. So grow together by affirming one another, being attentive to each other's emotional needs but don't be too absorbed in them.

Type 2 & Type 5: The old saying of "opposites attract" holds true with a Five. You're all warmth, comfort, communication, and caring, while Type Five is pretty much the opposite. Yet even with these differences, the Five's wisdom, commitment, and trustworthiness are very attractive to you. Fives pay great attention to detail, and once they "let in" a partner, they go all in. That makes you feel pretty special and important. The deep mystery and loyalty between the two sets you off on a lifelong journey to know more about each other and life. The greatest challenge is how you respond to stress and conflict. You're emotionally expressive, while the Five is calm and always rational. That can often leave you feeling like they are not as engaged in a conversation. You can be pretty overwhelming for a Type Five, causing them to walk away and isolate themselves for a while, often leaving you feeling abandoned and rejected. Grow together by realizing that you have some similarities in that you're both sensitive in your own way, and your needs aren't at odds with each other. Learn to work through your differences and find ways to communicate that don't overwhelm the Five while at the same time engaging enough for you to also feel understood.

Type 2 & Type 6: A relationship with a Six is deep, steadfast, loyal, and based on serving each other. Your empathetic and affectionate nature is very comforting to the Six because they feel like someone has their back at all times. They work hard at the relationship to create a sense of stability for you, which makes you feel prioritized and valued. Perhaps the best part about this relationship is the strong friendship that exists, which creates a kind of supportive, attentive, and responsible relationship that can be extremely fulfilling for you.

One of the challenges you may face with a Six is their subconscious tendency to test their partner. Sometimes they might just push you away and go cold for no reason. Their constant need to be reassured that you love and trust them might become overwhelming for you, especially if you feel like you've done everything possible to prove your love. On the other hand, the Six can easily misunderstand your constant prodding and overbearing help as being pushy and controlling. You like to "fix" things when you see a problem, but a Six tends to work through concerns by verbalizing them. So, grow together by continually working on your friendship & connection. Have an open dialogue regarding your needs and how you'd like those needs to be met.

Type 2 & Type 7: With a Type Seven, life is a never-ending adventure, and spontaneity is the norm. The energy, fun, enthusiasm, and pleasant nature that Type Seven radiates inspires you to become more in tune with your own desires. You bring generosity, empathy, and a concern for the welfare of others that grounds the Seven in healthy ways. It reminds them to slow down and pay attention to their loved ones. Your giving nature inspires the Seven to think about others more instead of always focusing on their own needs. You get to see how bold they are at chasing after their own dreams and thinking outside the box. That rubs off on you in positive ways.

One of the challenges you face in the relationship is the tension created by your emotional connection or lack thereof. From your point of view, Sevens isn't as present as you'd like them to be, especially when feelings come up and that can make you feel unseen. You might react to this by demanding that the Seven pay more attention to your needs or by trying to "fix" the Seven because you feel like they just need help to get better. In either case, the result is often more tension because the Seven often feel too caged or cornered and may run, fearing that they'll get trapped and lose their freedom. Grow together by prioritizing open dialogue. Don't repress or skim through conflict and unpleasant thoughts. Encourage your partner to face these unpleasant emotions courageously because it's part of a healthy human experience. Reassure one another of your commitment before wadding into difficult topics, then reward yourselves for having hard conversations.

Type 2 & Type 8: With an Eight, the attraction is strong because you see something in the other that's needed. The Eight needs the gentle, warm nature that it can protect, and you are deeply attracted to the power and tenacity you admire in the Eight. You soften some of the rough edges of the Eight. The Eight helps you set healthy boundaries and learn to boldly say NO! Together, you bring out the best in each other and become caring and passionate people.

A big challenge in this relationship is the difference in perspectives regarding defining independence. A Type Eight is guarded, self-reliant, and enjoys autonomy a lot, but as a Two, you're constantly seeking affection and affirmation. The Eight's independent streak can sometimes feel unloving because you'd rarely go off and do your own thing without considering your partner, yet that often happens to you. Suppose the relationship is between two average or unhealthy Enneagram types. In that case, things can get pretty ugly as both of you become overbearing and demanding. Grow together by embracing the safety, consistency, and security you provide for one another.

Type 2 & Type 9: With a Type Nine, the relationship is loving, warm, and serene. Things are comfortable and always easy going. The Nine is accepting and understanding and allows you the freedom to just be yourself. That helps you feel secure in the relationship because you feel loved without working for it. Your helpful, empathetic nature and the attention you give the Nine can help them tune in to their own desires and find their voice in the relationship.

A challenge you might experience in this relationship would be finding that balance between your active, action-oriented, and emotionally expressive nature and the Nine's relaxed way of moving through life. At times, your vibrant and helpful energy may become too much for the Nine. Because they don't like conflict, it can lead to avoidance and passive aggressive behavior. That can create distance between your relationship and cause you to become resentful and indignant.

AFFIRMATIONS FOR ENNEAGRAM TYPE 2

Affirmations can be a great tool when you begin replacing your negative thoughts and habits. Learn to become your own cheerlead and direct some of that tender loving care inward by speaking words that uplift and encourage you. Here is a list for you to try out.

- I am my best self when helping others.
- I love and approve of myself.
- I am worthy of all the love in the universe simply because I exist.
- I give and receive unconditional love.
- Loving others is easier when I love myself first.
- I know my true worth.
- I take time to tend to my own needs.

Remember, these affirmations only work if you feel and believe in what you're saying. Pick a few that resonate with you emotionally and use them as often as needed.

DAILY LIFESTYLE TIPS FOR GROWTH AND HAPPINESS

Invest time daily focusing on yourself

It's time to start investing time in your growth and development. The more you rise to healthier levels of development, the greater your impact will be on others. Ask yourself, "when was the last time I tended to my own needs and desires?" If you can't answer this question quickly, you need to self-reflect and take some new action. Make some adjustments and ask for help where needed so you can nurture yourself into a balanced life. Your giving should come from a place of overflow and unconditional love.

Open your mind to receive

It might seem easy to other people, but I know how hard this must be for you. Twos struggle with receiving because it appears selfish to ask another to do something for you. However, asking for help and opening your heart toward the kindness coming from others isn't selfish. It's an act of love. The more you cultivate your essential value of humility, the easier it will be to receive. To help your mind shift into openness, ask yourself the following questions. Will receiving this assistance or thing make the person providing it genuinely happy? Will loving myself help me interact with others on a more emotional level? Is it possible for me to experience the same joy while receiving that I do while giving?

Create a daily routine for self-care

Dear Two, it's essential to realize that your ability to help, support, and love others must come from a place of overflow, not co-dependency. The more you work on rising to higher and healthier levels of development, the more you'll see that you can't pour from an empty cup. Your cup must be filled to the brim first, so practicing self-care is imperative.

Some self-care rituals to integrate into your life include morning walks, yoga, personal development studies, and embodied meditations. You also want to pay more attention to your self-talk and the tone you use yourself. Ensure that inner dialogue carries the same compassion, love, and gentleness you extend to others. One last suggestion I can offer for self-care is to give yourself a treat regularly. If you enjoy massages or pedicures, give yourself a treat as often as possible. Remember, your friends and family love you for who you are, not because of your availability and hospitality.

Engage in some solo activities that you enjoy

Do you enjoy baking, cooking, painting, dancing, or poetry? Sign up for an in-person or virtual class and learn something new for yourself. Curl up with a new novel on a Saturday night or watch your favorite comedy in bed. Make a list of activities you can enjoy doing alone and use that time to just be in your own company. You'll be amazed at what transformation that can give you.

Practice mindfulness

Mindfulness is part of self-care practices and can include various activities, including mindfulness walks, meditation, gratitude practices, mindfulness eating, etc. Think of it like this - anytime you're practicing present moment awareness and fully engrossed in the activity at hand, you're tapping into mindfulness. Done each day consistently, you can experience new levels of self-love and self-acceptance, which are critical to the health of your mental, emotional and spiritual well-being.

Journal

Using a private journal to record your thoughts, express your emotions and practice gratitude is a powerful way to connect with your inner world. When journaling down your feelings, you create an outlet and a more objective way of recognizing what's really going on. It can enable you to see how you react to situations and the underlying thoughts so you can know what's driving your behavior. Another added benefit of journaling is practicing daily gratitude. The benefits of gratitude are widely known and scientifically proven, including lowering blood pressure, improving mood, and improving overall mental health. Practice gratitude daily, and you'll naturally feel more loved and loving.

CHAPTER 9
ENNEAGRAM TYPE 3
THE ACHIEVER OR PERFORMER

Over the following two chapters, we'll go in-depth on my favorite Type. The Enneagram Type Three is commonly referred to as the Achiever or performer. The title is quite fitting because, as Threes (yes, I am a Three), we are success-oriented, driven, and strive to be the best. Threes want to be significant and distinguished through their personal achievements. We must continue advancing and achieving in life because that adds to our sense of worth. It's easy to spot a Three because they are usually the confident, ambitious, image-conscious, and goal-oriented individual in the group who isn't afraid to speak up. Threes tend to be quite charming, attractive, eloquent, energetic, diplomatic, and poised. When operating at higher levels of development, a Type Three is authentic, self-accepting, inspirational, and makes a great role model for others.

An essential defining quality of a Three is this innate desire to achieve great things in life. Threes dream big, make a plan, and then take massive actions toward said goals. If you're a three, your word and reputation matter, and you consider these priceless assets. It's essential to leave a mark on any project you work on, and you want to be remembered for being unique. People look up to you, and you like that, so you keep pushing people forward, motivating them to succeed. You've got a natural knack for identifying people's strengths and weaknesses. That enables you to place people in positions that are more likely to succeed.

In the Enneagram system, Threes are one of the most successful and popular personalities because they naturally have high self-assuredness and work extra hard to build on their skills and talents.

Many Threes who aren't yet operating at higher and healthier levels of development struggle with workaholism and competitiveness, which can become detrimental to their well-being and relationships. They might get trapped into being to image consciousness and trying to keep up a status that others admire even when things aren't going right, which can take a toll on them. This need to look good and save face creates a lot of pressure for average and unhealthy Threes, leading to a downward spiral and inner disconnect. When that natural energy is out of control and negative, Threes can be highly destructive. The average and unhealthy Three may appear malicious, self-absorbed, self-aggrandizing, narcissistic, and even untrustworthy from an outside observer. That's why we need to work on rising higher in our development.

STRENGTHS OF A THREE

Threes are self-starters and very intelligent. They constantly search for ways to improve and get better at their game. While each individual will have their definition of success, for most

Threes, success is about having the finer things in life, being surrounded by the right kind of people, and being around power. To have all these, Threes go the extra mile each day and leverage their strengths which include some of the following:

- Adaptability and quickly pivoting in situations so they can keep moving in the direction of the target.
- A charisma and enthusiasm that's contagious and attractive.
- Commitment and dedication to goal achievement.
- Being open to new opportunities and unafraid of responsibility and accountability.
- Strong will, ability to think critically, and act pragmatically.

Key personality traits of Type Three

- Charisma
- Focus
- Productive and efficient
- Intense work ethic

Common hobbies for a Type Three

- Dancing
- Modeling
- Singing
- Competitive sports
- Developing talents

FEARS AND WEAKNESSES

By now, it's evident that one of the distinguishing expressions of Type Three is the need to accomplish great things and be greatly admired and loved for all their achievements. A Threes biggest fear is to be worthless, insignificant, and a failure.

What's the Basic Fear driving this behavior? The fear of being worthless or without inherent value. For many Type Threes, there's a subconscious belief that to be loved and worthy in the eyes of others, they must succeed or at least appear successful. Deep down, all they want is to ve valuable, and so Threes do anything and everything to demonstrate that. Many times, this basic fear is expressed in one of two ways. The first is through constant activity. Always doing anything and everything to move the needle. The second is through emotional neglect. I can attest to both things because I struggled with hyperactivity for a long time. I adapted my life to meeting certain expectations that I perceived would enable me to maintain a particular image of success. I would engage in projects I didn't even enjoy or care about just because I thought it would bring more achievement and recognition. And when projects weren't that good, I dropped them quickly because I didn't want those failures to hurt my image. The other issue I had was dealing with my emotions. I always tried to put them on hold or stuff them on the back burner as much as possible because "I didn't have time" to deal with them. But the truth is that I just didn't want to deal with my feelings. If these are struggles you've had, keep reading because I'll show you how to move past this level of development.

DESIRES AND MOTIVATIONS

The Basic Desire for a Type Three is to feel valuable and worthwhile. Threes want to be accepted, loved, and desirable. Now, I know what you're thinking. Isn't that a selfish desire? If you're a Three, you understand that it's anything but selfish. This overwhelming care to be valuable and desired translates into the desire to help others. I can confidently say that I am eager and driven to help others as much as I want to help myself. After all, helping others means I get to fulfill my own goals. Many Threes are doing this unconsciously because they innately know that the more they lift others up, the higher they will rise. The respect and admiration we crave are earned. We're not afraid to work for it. Of course, when dealing with unhealthy levels of development, that craving to be successful does turn dark. It may involve deceit, manipulation, and other means that may not be for the highest good of anyone. But when dealing with healthy Threes, success means success for everyone around them.

Core values

- Productivity
- Goal-oriented, results-oriented
- Personal growth
- Competency
- Respect
- Adaptability, Flexibility
- Prestige, Reputation

Type Three celebrities and famous people you might know to include American talk show host, author, actress, and entrepreneur Oprah Winfrey, Actor, rapper Will Smith, Former

Pro NBA superstar, and Entrepreneur Michael Jordan, and Actor Tom Cruise.

Wondering if you could be a Type Three? Here are some personality indicators

1. Winning is everything. You need to win and be the best at whatever you've set your mind on.
2. You're internally driven and motivated to be productive.
3. You hate and possibly even fear failure as it goes against your primary desire.
4. You care deeply about your image. Even at healthy levels, Threes still care about how they present themselves to the world.
5. Your vision of what you want is clear, and you're consistently thinking about the future and how it could be better.
6. You're a natural leader and find it easy to motivate, inspire and lead others into their greatness.
7. You love setting big goals, accomplishing them, and doing it all over again.
8. It's a struggle for you to have downtime and just unwind, especially when you've got an exciting goal on your mind.
9. You have a hard time celebrating your successes. You're already chasing the next big project as soon as you hit a target.
10. You have the natural ability to read a room and adapt to fit the audience you want to win over. That gives you the edge over others and makes it easy to build connections with almost anyone.

YOUR WINGS

Wings are the numbers adjacent to your primary Enneagram number. As a Three, you have

- The Enneagram Three with a Two-Wing: "The Charmer"
- The Enneagram Three with a Four-Wing: "The Professional"

While you may have tendencies that lean into both wings, you'll likely be more dominant in one than the other. That will become your Dominant Wing. The Charmer, aka enchanter, is highly personable, extroverted, caring, and compassionate. They will be more community-oriented and passionate about community development. Although goal-oriented like any other Three, the charmer is more invested in making relationships succeed and motivating others into greatness.

The Professional (sometimes referred to as the expert) is highly success-driven and more focused on personal goals rather than communal ones. They tend to have strict and clearly defined boundaries between the various parts of their lives, such as work, friendship, etc., and they generally like to be admired from afar. This particular Three is more in tune with their emotions. Unlike the charmer, they have a closer-knit friend and family group.

Meaning of your Wing

If you're a 3w2(Three with Two-Wing), you're naturally people-oriented and genuinely care about building relationships. Sure, you're still highly image-conscious, success-driven ambitious, but you have the added benefit of not needing to over-extend yourself or "fake it" when it comes to relationships. Your efforts and desire to accomplish greatness are intensely focused on family, friends, and the community you care about. In other words, you're likely pouring more of your energy into relationship success rather than worldly success.

Type 3w2 are drawn to careers that offer authority and the opportunity for advancement. Their competitiveness often means they'll thrive in fields where this aspect of their personality is an asset rather than a hindrance. That includes:

- Lawyer
- Journalist
- Politician
- Event planner
- Television anchor
- Advertising consultant
- Entrepnreneur

Welcome to my world. If you're a 3w4 (Three with Four-Wing), then your personality type is one of the more complex ones. As a Three with a Four Wing, our personality is a bit contradictory because, on the one hand, we can be chameleons, changing color to blend in whenever we feel the need to. But with a dominant Four Wing, authenticity is a massive influence. Finding that alignment between being a Three and the strong urge to be authentically myself has been one of the most challenging aspects of my self-discovery journey. So if it gets scary and hard as you go through this, rest easy. You're not alone. The intention is to grow in your development to the point where your focus shifts from superficial to meaningful things where you can leverage all your natural abilities, including that perceptive shape-shifting gift.

As a type 3w4, certain roles will be better suited for your personality, including:

- Lawyer
- Financial analyst
- Architect
- Publicist
- Venture capitalist
- Marketer
- Investment banker
- Politician

The Arrows and what they mean

Your Enneagram personality type is linked to two other points worth discussing. These lines are called arrows, and each indicates how you show up at your best and worst. That simply means you get to learn the full spectrum of your personality and the best path towards growth, alerting you to the red flags you need to become aware of so you can pause, step back and avoid crashing and burning again. One arrow is called the Arrow of Disintegration, which shows our stress number. The other is called the Arrow of Integration.

For us as Threes, we have 9 as the arrow of Disintegration and 6 as the arrow of Integration. When we move toward the unhealthy path of Disintegration, we take on traits from an unhealthy Nine because our dominant need for attention and significance has been challenged. That might express itself as withdrawal, anxiety, fear, and uncertainty. If you've ever faced too much pressure at work and fell into overwhelm, guilt for not meeting your goals, or anger towards everyone, that was you on the path of Disintegration. Many unhealthy Threes on this path will drink excessively, become overly aggressive and engage in all kinds of substance abuse to cope.

On the other hand, when we move toward Integration, we cultivate and activate the healthier qualities of a Six. That causes us to move through situations and life feeling more secure and accepting of ourselves and others. We no longer feel the need to be validated by others because we are content with who we are and the life choices we've made. By developing more traits of a healthy Six, we become more focused and forgiving. We set clear boundaries that enable us to take care of our emotional needs. To understand the relationship of these arrows and how we came about with healthy and unhealthy levels, let's talk about Type Three's various levels of development.

THE 9 LEVELS OF DEVELOPMENT, FROM LOWEST TO HIGHEST

Levels of Development arise from Riso and Hudson's teachings and the founders of the Enneagram Institute, which is a great place to take your Enneagram Test. Their theory posits that all individuals fall into one of nine levels of functioning. The lowest level is nine, and the highest is level one. The levels are divided into a triad that subcategorizes these levels as healthy (1,2,3), average levels (4,5,6), and unhealthy levels (7,8,9).

Unhealthy

Level 9: This is the darkest, lowest, and most dangerous level an adult could live from for any Enneagram number. It's okay at infancy to be here—in fact, this is where we all start when we are infants. However, many adults have never developed past this stage or, even worse, keep falling back to this level. For Type Threes who are ambitious and image- and status-conscious, being at this level is highly destructive for them and those around them. At this stage of a Three's development, they are vindictive, relentless, and obsessive about destroying whatever reminds them of their own shortcomings and failures. The person will likely exhibit psychopathic behavior, generally displaying Narcissistic Personality Disorder.

Level 8: At this unhealthy level, the Three has developed a little, but is still stuck in harmful levels of expression, so they are highly devious and deceptive. The individual at this level will do anything to cover up their mistakes and failures because they want to keep that front that they are winning in life. This Three is also delusionally jealous of others, untrustworthy, malicious, and tends to sabotage and betray people if that's what it takes to win.

Level 7: This Three struggles mostly with fear of failure and is driven by that innate urge to avoid failure. Usually, that means doing whatever it takes to win and preserve their illusion of superiority. The individual at this level isn't really successful, but they "fake" things in their world to appear more successful than they really are. That makes them highly opportunistic and exploitative, seeking to covet the success of others at any chance they get.

Average

Level 6: At this level, the Enneagram Three has developed enough to rise to average levels of expression. This Three is self-focused, arrogant, grandiose, narcissistic, and has inflated notions about their success and talents. The struggle with jealousy is still prevalent, and they do anything to impress others with their superiority. It's easy to spot this Three because they are always the loudest in the room, trying to show others that they are the best even though they don't believe it.

Level 5: At this average level, Type Three is more concerned about accomplishing as much as possible and winning the admiration of others. On a more positive note, this Three is pragmatic and efficient. They are solely focused on crushing their goal and getting what they want. Being intimate with another or "letting anyone in" is a challenge. The smooth facade used to win over people keeps them out of tune with their authentic self, and they avoid dealing with their feelings.

Level 4: This Type Three is career and performance-focused. They want to be the best and constantly strive to achieve bigger and bigger goals. Fear of failure is still a considerable challenge. At times, they may compare themselves to others who are more successful.

Healthy

Level 3: The rise in development for Type Three to this healthy phase is liberating. While the Three is still ambitious, striving to become outstanding and the best they can be, they are more geared toward becoming an exceptional human and not just winning in their career. This three works hard to embody widely admired qualities and invests a lot in personal growth. They are also highly effective, and others naturally follow and get motivated by being around this individual.

Level 2: At this level, Type Three is self-assured, desirable, charming, gracious, adaptable, and possesses high levels of self-esteem. They are competent and believe in themselves and the value they bring to the table.

Level 1: This is the highest and most advanced level that a Three can hope to attain. At this level, transcendence has occurred, and the Three truly is operating at their best (in complete alignment with their divine Self). They are authentic, self-accepting, gentle, benevolent, modest, and full of heart in all they do. People love and follow this individual.

TYPE THREE'S PASSION

The Enneagram identifies the Passion or vice of a Three as deceit or, better said - vanity and false self-image. I view the Passion as our ego's primary coping tool to reconnect with essence. Although it's not the best path and often leads to Disintegration and unhealthy habits, the underlying intention is to find our way back home. Usually, this Passion is born out of childhood experiences or some wound that caused us to wear a mask and protect ourselves from the world. The more we wore this mask, the harder it became to recognize our true self. As members of the Heart Triad, losing our essence and true self meant we also lost touch with our emotions and the innate joy and love we know we deserve. So in an attempt to have some of that feeling of wholeness, we tend to deceive ourselves and others. For a Three, the passion of deceit is expressed in the attitudes and behavior of becoming what others admire and desire. It can be in the form of mimicking another person, promoting personal success over all else while ignoring failures, disguising perceived flaws, and being overly obsessed with image and status. Take a moment now to candidly reflect on the following questions:

- Do I believe that I have to earn love by being worthy?
- Do I tend to shape-shift and become what others want me to be just to get what I want?
- Am I overly identified with my personality and outer image?
- Do I often take on the ideas of others, especially role models, and wear them as my personal identity?

The honest response you get from this simple exercise will move you toward your virtue and a step closer to your true essence. What is virtue? Your virtue represents your most accurate, most authentic expression of yourself. It's typically the exact opposite of your Passion or ego fixation. For a Three, that virtue is Truth and Integrity. And it expresses itself in behavior as:

- becoming authentically yourself without regarding what others think
- slowing down frequently to acknowledge and process your emotions
- becoming more self-accepting and content to just be yourself
- feeling whole and confident in your Truth

CHILDHOOD AND EMOTIONAL PATTERNS OF TYPE THREE

Emotional patterns for an adult are often shaped by early childhood experiences and how one interprets their upbringing. Each of us has a filter through which we understand the world around us. For Enneagram Threes, that filter is associated with external success. As children, Threes were deeply connected to the nurturing figure in their life and learned to intuit that person's needs before they were expressly stated. In my case, it was my mother, and I did everything possible to meet those needs because there was no "man of the house," and I needed to step in to fill the gap left by that protective presence. Some Threes were part of a big family and didn't receive the attention they needed, so they used performance to stand out and get attention. I also have Type Threes friends who grew up with amazing parents who praised them for their accomplishments. So as kids, they learned to associate love with "doing" instead of "being."

All Threes strive to win or accomplish something because we get that look of approval we've loved receiving since childhood. It doesn't matter what kind of a family set-up you had. If the messaging your brain received is that winning gets you love and attention, you do whatever it takes to keep that reality going. That could have been in sports, academics, and even a career now that you're an adult.

There's nothing wrong with wanting to win and succeed in life but where things get tricky is when it's founded on a false sense of self. Suppose you're only going after success in life because you've attached that to your self-worth and love. In that case, you're dealing with the fear of rejection and abandonment. That's what the Enneagram is attempting to help you uncover so that you can heal those emotional wounds and live your ambitious life from a place of wholeness. Instead of using external accomplishments and successes as distractions and masks to cover up the disconnect from your true Self, make the shift and heal from the inside out. Let's get a little granular on your particular personality type by discussing the subtypes to enable this transformation. Then we'll cover lifestyle tips and changes you can integrate.

SUBTYPES FOR TYPE THREE

The Enneagram profiling system allows for 3 subtypes in each Type. These are Self-Preservation, Social, and One-to-One (Sexual) variants. Remember, all three instinctual variants exist in all of us. Still, the order in which they stack up determines their influence on our lives. One will be most dominant and the easiest for you to resonate with and observe as behavior and thought patterns in your life. The second will feel a little neutral and less influential, and the third will be the least significant. The third instinct becomes a blind spot for many because it's totally underdeveloped and out of their conscious recognition. Depending on which instinct is most dominant will shape your unique personality and how you approach life as a Three.

Self-Preservation Three (SP)

Security is the main focus for this Enneagram Three, which is also the countertype of the group. As the countertype, this Three will act in ways that make it easy to mistype the SP Three. SP Threes have boundless energy and high drive, which they use to accomplish personal goals like buying lovely homes and establishing financial security. Unlike classic Threes, this individual dislikes being a show-off. They prefer not to advertise their accomplishments and strengths.

While they still value winning and looking good, they don't want to be seen as image-oriented. Don't get me wrong, this Three wishes to be recognized for their hard work and excellence but not in the vain and often materialistic way other Threes enjoy.

This subtype is reliable, efficient, and productive and aspires to do the right thing for themselves and others. Their pursuit of security and self-sufficiency through hard work may lead to struggles with workaholism.

Social Three (SO)

Prestige is the main focus for this individual. Driven by the vain need to look good, impress others, and get the job done, Social Threes enjoy being on stage in the spotlight. Social Threes know how to climb the social ladder and achieve success. Of all the subtypes, Social Threes are the most aggressive and competitive. Success and gaining influence are critical to these Threes and may even cut corners or cover up failure as long as they get the desired outcome.

Sexual/ One-to-One Three (SX)

Charisma is the main focus for this Threes, and it's expressed in how much time, energy, and attention they place on their physical appearance. While this Three isn't as obvious and overt about their vanity as in the case of a Social Three, they are also not in denial in conflict with it as is the case with the Self-preservation Three. Their vanity and personal attractiveness are employed to make others feel good. Sexual Threes have a harder time talking about themselves and often put the focus on the people they want to promote. There are some people-pleasing tendencies in a Sexual Three, especially around family, friends, or team members that they care about. It can be easy to mistype this subtype Three as a Two because they tend to think and act along the lines of "If those around me achieve success, then I am more successful."

CHAPTER 10

WORK AND LIFESTYLE TIPS FOR TYPE 3S

There's a lot to cover about the growth opportunities for all Enneagram Threes. Before that, let's address some of the struggles you'll face at some point in your journey. The battles are already a present-day reality for some of my readers. They might be avoiding this topic altogether. If that's you, it's time to face the demons and put them to rest.

STRUGGLES OF AN ENNEAGRAM TYPE 3

The feeling that success is always out of reach

That is a feeling every Three can relate to somehow, mainly when operating at average or unhealthy levels of development. The person works hard to climb the ladder and hit the target, but it's an ever-moving target. And if you look around, there's always someone more skilled, successful, famous, better looking, etc. For average and unhealthy Threes, this ever-moving target causes them to feel unsuccessful and worthless, so they need to keep upgrading and reaching for the next best thing. When handled poorly, this feeling becomes a breeding ground for a lot of pain and lack of gratitude.

What to do: Let's spend a few moments writing down your goals over the next year, five years, and ten years respectively. Are those goals really yours? Did you pick them because you're trying to compete with someone or prove something to someone? Do you have any goals you chose because you feel achieving them will enable you to become the highest and best version of yourself? What would you have as goals over the next year if there were no rewards and people loved you for yourself?

Comparisons

Another unhelpful behavior for average and unhealthy Threes is the habit of comparing their success to the successes of others. No matter how good they get, if they feel someone else has it better, they immediately feel insecure. When around people less success-ful, they feel proud and competent but perhaps bored because there's no challenge. It takes a lot of personal growth to shed this habit of comparison and stop feeling insecure when around more successful people.

What to do: Consider doing activities that take you out of that competitive mindset and enable you to see that you're on a unique path, and so is everyone else. You could even collaborate on a charitable activity like cooking for kids with special needs or building an educational facility for a local school (with the people you tend to compare yourself with). It's important to realize that your success is yours, and no one can take it away from you. And the same is true for the people around you. The scarcity mindset of comparison is more hurtful than helpful to your success on this abundant planet.

Always being "on."

This is super common across the board for Threes because we just don't know how to "unwind." In fact, many Threes hate that word. The lower the level of development (average and unhealthy levels), the more problematic this becomes because this tendency leads to vanity, false images, and exaggerations. When a Three starts to "fake it," whether emotionally, physically, or through their status, just to appear like they're "on," that's a big issue. Because it only amplifies their hidden insecurities and forces them to overextend themselves trying to save face.

What to do: It's okay to be enthusiastic, energetic, and always on as long as it comes from an authentic place. Make sure you're in control of that "on" switch.

Burnout

Another significant struggle for average and unhealthy Threes is overworking to the point of a breakdown. Because the person tends to get too obsessed with success and goal achievement, they can quickly fall out of touch with their physical and emotional needs. That leads to sleep debt, poor diet, lack of exercise, and overall health issues from self-neglect. Threes can easily over-extend themselves in the name of making dreams come true. The other area they often neglect is their relationships. When focused on a goal, they'll ignore everything and everyone, including loved ones, if they don't see how the relationship is helping them achieve their goal.

What to do: Prioritize your self-care routine. Do a daily check-in with yourself to ensure everything is okay internally. Stop and take deep breaths every so often. Give yourself permission to nap, eat lunch and dinner in peace, take long walks, etc. Plan your busy schedule accordingly so you can have ample sleep each night and include some family and social life every so often to give the people in your life a little attention and affection.

Feeling unloved and struggling with self-acceptance and self-love

This is the holy grail for a Three. The journey to self-discovery isn't to make your ambitions and desires a bad thing but rather to enable you to experience true and unconditional love. That love comes from within by learning to accept and love yourself first. Then allow others to love you. I know this is hard and definitely requires some serious self-development. Still, once you get it, you'll no longer fixate on perfecting your outer image or impressing people.

The awards, fancy cars, homes, and social status will be nice to have, but they won't define you. The struggle for love started at a young age. Most Threes felt unloved for who they were and, in turn, grew into people who cage their emotions and strive for achievement. It's a survival mechanism that served its purpose. If you want to express and experience the highest and best version of your life, it's time to shed this belief and find your true self.

What to do: Invest time getting to know who you really are. Partake in some self-love activities, read a book or attend a seminar that introduces you to the aspects of you that are beyond what you know. Once you know who you really are, beyond your ego-personality, you will learn to love and accept yourself. This may take time, but the more you move in this direction, the sooner you'll find your "lost self."

OPPORTUNITIES FOR GROWTH

Let's uncover some of the ways you can start growing personally and professionally now that you're doing the inner work of moving to higher levels of development.

Develop the intention to accept and love yourself

You can shift into more positive traits by challenging your current value system. Choose to stop relying on achievement and recognition. According to Enneagram teachings, the integrated path of growth is influenced by the Enneagram Six. So as a Three moving into higher levels of development, these lines of growth Influenced by Six will enable you to realize that your value isn't determined by other people. Their approval or lack thereof has nothing to do with your self-worth. You still possess tremendous value whether you're winning accolades or not. This growth path helps you embrace who you really are, and you become more honest, authentic, and loyal to your true self.

Practice active listening

As a Three, I can attest that listening to other people's advice isn't easy. I've trained myself to develop this quality because it is essential. Our stubborn nature tends to be at odds with other people's suggestions of how things should be done. When working in a team environment or even with a spouse, allowing two-way communication is healthy and critical to thriving relationships. This is an area of growth for all Type Three, so be gentle with yourself and notice each time you shut down someone's ideas because your mind is already made up. Learning to listen to other people's ideas and their side of the story gives you a broader perspective and makes you seem less self-centered.

Shedding the urge to lie

The core Passion or sin for a Type Three is deceit. The higher up your development you rise, the easier it will be to resist the temptation to deceive, lie or twist things around to your advantage. As you find your authentic self and reconnect with that higher version of you, vanity and deceit will naturally fade away. You won't feel the constant need to maintain a false image or wear a deceptive mask.

Let's get something straight. Achieving success and following your ambitions and dreams is right, and it's wonderful to desire a better lifestyle, that eight-figure income, and global travel for yourself. Just don't "chase" after these things to impress others or as a coping mechanism to hide your shame. If the success you seek is only a shell to cover feelings of emptiness, then no growth occurs. Heal the inside first, find who you really are, and then make manifest whatever feels right to your Higher Self.

Give back to your community

Find a cause within your community that resonates with you. Making contributions to society can be a great way to train yourself to share the spotlight and see abundance at different levels of life. Your perspective of success will expand as you interact with others totally different from you and yet successful in their own right.

We associate success with power, material accomplishments, and status as Threes. Success in this new discovery expands to other areas as well. You'll learn to embrace teamwork and altruism, and it's a great way to inspire and take care of the people in your community. Consider volunteering for a project or activities that resonate with you.

ENNEAGRAM TYPE 3 UNDER STRESS

When Type Threes get stressed, we become disconnected and fall into average and unhealthy levels. We express behavior that's typically influenced by the arrow Nine. When that happens, things take a downward spiral because, as you can imagine, being influenced by the poor qualities of an Enneagram Nine like procrastination, slothfulness, and indifference spell doom for our typically high-energy personality. So you'll sense a disconnect within yourself and realize that you're getting caught up in busy work that means nothing to you and doesn't really move the needle in your life. You'll also start putting things on hold, and feelings of apathy will increase exponentially.

As Threes, we get really stressed out by some of the following:

- Feeling incompetent about something we care about.
- Being around incompetent people.
- Losing
- Not seeing progress toward a set objective or goal.
- Being around people who lack vision.
- Not being recognized for our hard work and accomplishments.
- Feeling undesirable or worthless.
- Not being challenged enough.

How to ease your back into a healthy state:

The best way to shift from that paralyzing, unhealthy state of stress and Disintegration is to recognize that you're behaving like an unhealthy Nine. And just pause and take some time to decompress and let out the stuff weighing you down. Find someone you can trust and tell them what's going on and why you're so stressed. If you don't trust anyone, consider journaling everything in a private journal. What matters is that you recognize that it's happening and immediately release it from your system.

Take deep breaths and tune into your body. What's going on there? Are you tired? Hungry? In pain? What could you do for your body now to bring it into a state of ease and good health? Once you've let out the stress either verbally or through journaling and taken care of your bodily needs, shift your attention to something creative that you can do to start a new momentum. For most Threes, creative expression comes easy. There's always something we enjoy doing, such as writing, drawing, painting, playing an instrument, pottery, listening to music, etc. You already know your thing, so block out time immediately and engage in this activity until it consumes you and shifts your energy. Now that you've got a new momentum started keep adding activities to build on it until you get back on track.

RELATIONSHIPS

Type Threes are naturally energetic, devoted, and value genuine care. When it comes to personal and professional relationships, a Three typically assumes a competitive, ally, or mentoring role with the other person. Where they position you determines how your relationship plays out.

In romantic relationships, Threes usually seek partners capable of bringing something unique and beneficial to the relationship. Depending on the level of development, the Three will be drawn to different qualities in the other, whether that is intelligence, mutual interests, or support of some kind. In the workplace, Threes are attracted to the people who can grant them access to attain their chosen objective. Depending on the situation, that could be the manager, an executive, or the company owner. When less healthy, Threes become too preoccupied with achievement and success, sometimes at the expense of the people around them. That's why it's essential to become self-aware and keep creating that balance as a Three so that your loved ones don't feel neglected or lose interest in being part of your journey.

RELATIONSHIP TIPS WITH OTHER TYPES

As a Three, you desire someone who will love and appreciate you, compliment or match your intensity and keep you challenged in all the right ways. Here are some ways to improve your relationships with other Enneagram Types.

Type 3 & Type 1: You have a partner that genuinely supports your endeavors with a Type One. Someone who also believes just as you do that staying rational is the best way to deal with conflict and figure things out. The One admires your can-do attitude and the fact that you always get things done. You appreciate Type One's commitment, sense of responsibility, and high standards. When both of you operate at higher levels of development, this can be a beautiful relationship.

Some of the challenges you might face together is stepping out of that serious, strict, task-oriented mindset and into friendship and romance. The One might also see your shape-shifting as manipulative and shallow, while you might see the One's principled approach to everything, including date night, as too rigid, dull, and stifling.

You can grow together by softening each other's edginess and learning what it truly means to rest, relax and reset. Practice this in your relationship.

Type 3 & Type 2: You're a charming, passionate couple with a Type Two. The Two brings a lot of warmth, acceptance, and affirmation to your world, which you love. You bring the ambition, energy, and liveliness that inspires the Two to follow their dreams. There's plenty of attention, affection, and interpersonal connection when operating at healthy levels between you and your partner. It's easy to maintain healthy, positive social engagements. Your combined attractiveness and confidence radiate dynamic energy that people can't help but admire.

Some of the challenges you might face include a lack of understanding of your own feelings. Sure, you can pick up on the other person's energy and feelings but are you investing enough time to do the same with your inner feelings? When there's inner self-neglect, the relationship faces many issues. You might feel overwhelmed by the Two's helpfulness and desire for emotional connection, especially when under stress. The Two can feel neglected as you drown in your ambition and tasks.

You can grow together by learning to have an open dialogue with high-quality questions that enable you to reflect on what's really going on inside. Get in touch with your own feelings first. It will enrich your relationships far more than any therapy.

Type 3 & Type 3: With another Three as your partner, it's like being with a perfect mirror that enables you to do extraordinary things together. You bring out the best in each other. You're charming, successful, and pleasant, and you just get each other. A pair of Threes in a relationship means both parties understand the importance of being outstanding and admired. Yet beneath all that, you still get to see behind the mask and realize there's a caring, genuine and loving person underneath all that hard work and great ambition.

While I think Threes in a relationship is a match made in heaven, the best time to be in a relationship with another Three is at higher levels of development. Otherwise, the challenge you'll face is hitting a wall with your partner when they get worn out from the busy demanding schedule you both run. With such hectic days and big ambitions driving both of you, it's easy to neglect feelings or downtime together. That tends to create gaps in your relationship, and you'll often find yourselves caught up in opposite cycles of achievement and exhaustion. The fact that you don't like to admit failure or even apologize when something is your fault can also become a huge issue.

Grow together by prioritizing the "feelings" part of your relationship as much as everything else. Train yourself to sit with the discomfort of dealing with emotions until it stops being too uncomfortable. When you feel like withdrawing, make an effort to do the opposite and communicate with your partner. Realize that apologizing isn't a sign of failure or weakness.

Type 3 & Type 4: With a Type Four, the relationship is earnest and intense and facilitates plenty of open communication. The Four brings introspection, depth, and meaning to the relationship, which is excellent for you because it helps you slow down and do your inner work. Your ambition, energy, and structure are desirable to the Four. It helps them become more present in the world and increase their self-confidence. The relationship is very balanced, and you become more sensitive and comfortable expressing yourself.

The main challenge you might face with a Four is how different their emotional temperaments are to you. You might find too much "emotion" to be overwhelming or irrational. They might see you as "fake" or apathetic because you just don't get as emotional about things as they do. In other words, sometimes you just don't understand them, and they feel the same about you.

Grow together by setting realistic expectations in your relationship. When tension arises, meet it head on as soon as you notice its ugly head. Be open and clear about how far you're willing to go to prioritize your partner's emotional needs and allow them to speak their heart. Listen with your head and heart if you truly want to maintain that long-lasting connection.

Type 3 & Type 5: With a Five, your relationship is efficient and stable. You both shine as you become more inventive and competent together. The Five bring creativity, depth, and objectivity to the relationship. They admire the work you put in to be the best at what you do because that's something they value. Your energy, confidence, and sociability is also very attractive to the Five and helps the Five out of their shell. When your assertiveness is combined with your partner's thoughtfulness and penchant for thorough research, the relationship brims with a dynamic steadiness that keeps you wanting more.

A common challenge you'll face is how you operate things and move through life. Fives tend to move at a thoughtful pace. Their measured approach helps them conserve energy, remaining steady and poised. As a Three, you're always thinking on your feet, so the speed is the name of your game. That can often create frustration, primarily if you're operating at average and unhealthy levels. You may feel like you're in a tug-of-war pulling in opposite directions.

Grow together by being open-minded enough to learn from the other. Get in touch with your feelings in a meaningful way and talk about them together. Work on rising to higher levels of development as partners.

Type 3 & Type 6: With a Six, you have a transparent, stable relationship that's resilient. The Six is encouraging, faithful, dutiful, and knows how to keep you grounded and encouraged. You know how to bring out the best in people, so as you highlight the good in your partner, they feel more encouraged to pursue their passions. The relationship is comfortable and makes it easy for you to find an emotional connection with your partner. With high levels of responsibility and hard work, you become unstoppable once you trust each other.

The main challenge you may encounter is the difference in fundamental values. A Six values loyalty above all else, and your shape-shifting tendencies can cause them to doubt your trustworthiness. They are also pretty cautious, which may conflict with your hard driving, less careful personality. And sometimes, you may feel like they're holding you back.

Work through your feelings as a couple. You can grow together by validating one another's focus of attention and staying present in the relationship. Keep an open dialogue and let your partner know that you respect their values even though how you express trustworthiness may not be what they're used to.

Type 3 & Type 7: There's never a dull moment in the relationship with a seven. Sevens are adventurous, courageous, and vibrant, which is excellent because that fun, spontaneous energy keeps things interesting for a Three. You are able to help the Seven become more focused, sensitive, and poised. It's a fun-filled, high-energy relationship.

The challenge you might face is the emotional neglect and avoidance that may build up over time. You tend to be busy, and Sevens don't like confrontation or negativity, so they might let things slide, creating gaps in your relationship. Your partner might also get frustrated with your constant desire for productivity. Because you're both sensitive to feelings of loss or rejection, it's likely that you'll quit avoiding abandonment.

Grow together by sharing your feelings and making time for open dialogue, even the uncomfortable stuff. Learn to slow down every once in a while.

Type 3 & Type 8: You're in for an intense, lively relationship with a Type Eight. The Eight brings just as much, if not more, assertiveness and passion, which is great because it allows you to be the fullest version of yourself without judgment. You help your partner let go of the need to control everything because they feel you're competent, responsible, and powerful enough to be trusted. It moves them out of that "lone wolf" energy, trying to do everything alone. It's a powerful, influential relationship, and you can build a solid unbreachable fort together.

The challenge, of course, is how extreme both your personalities are. Just as you match each other in positive ways, you also match each other in tension and conflict. Eights fear being vulnerable or betrayed, and given how easily you can shape-shift, that can cause alarm for a Type Eight. You may also struggle to deal with your partner's anger issues.

Grow together by letting go and working on your trust level. Have fun and allow yourself to be in situations where you're not in total control.

Type 3 & Type 9: With a Nine, you're in a serene, purposeful, easy-going relationship. Nines offer love, acceptance, and a sense of calm which makes you feel that they love you just for being. You give them the encouragement they need to find their voice and follow their dreams because you can see untapped potential. The relationship is very reciprocal, balanced, steady, and peaceful. You are each other's cheerleaders.

The main challenge you might face is conflicting energies. You might feel like the Nine is holding you back and your partner may feel neglected because you're always busy chasing after the next big goal. There's also the issue of procrastination and inaction that Nines often fall into, which can be utterly frustrating for you.

However, pushing your partner to take action leads to withdrawal and suppressed resentment.

You can grow together by listening to each other more with an open mind. If your partner says you need to slow down a little, remember it's well-intended. There may be some truth in their concern.

AFFIRMATIONS FOR ENNEAGRAM TYPE 3

Affirmations can be a great tool when you begin replacing your negative thoughts and habits. Learn to become your own cheer-lead and direct some of that tender loving care inward by speaking words that uplift and encourage you. Here is a list to help you out.

- I am more patient and find my own flow in life.
- I accept and love myself.
- I am full of energy and life.
- I allow myself to breathe and relax.
- I embrace myself despite my mistakes and imperfections.
- I am grateful for all my successes.
- I embrace leadership centered on truth, integrity, and compassion.
- I am authentic.

Remember, these affirmations only work if you feel and believe in what you're saying. Pick a few that resonate with you emotionally and use them as often as needed.

DAILY LIFESTYLE TIPS FOR GROWTH AND HAPPINESS

Schedule some regular time to unplug and reset

Our work is vital to us, and no one is asking you to give up on what you believe in. However, it's good for your mental, emotional, physical, and spiritual well-being to have some periods of rest and relaxation. That doesn't mean spending weeks lying on a hammock doing nothing (that would drive me crazy). It means figuring out what helps you feel relaxed and rested and adding that to your schedule as part of your downtime. Creating space to "unplug" from the world and daily demands is good. Find ways you enjoy unplugging. For me, it's going for a swim. I take laps each day before heading home for the evening. No phone, no people, just me and the water for 30min. That resets me.

Practice mindfulness

You can practice mindfulness eating, take mindful showers, or even take a yoga/meditation class if that resonates with you. Learning to be more mindful will also improve your ability to be present in each moment.

Focus on a relationship you care about

Your schedule is hectic, and there's barely enough time to get everything done. I get that. But if you have a few people in your life who matter to you, figure out a way to give them the attention and love they deserve. You can choose to focus on improving one relationship at a time. Prioritize some time this week to interact with someone you love. Be present during the interaction and show them how much you love and appreciate them. Communicate your feelings and let them know you're working hard to be more involved in the relationship. Then next week or next month, add one more person to your list. Relationships are critical to our success, so we need to figure out a way to prioritize them in our pursuit of success.

Keep a gratitude journal

I take five minutes daily to write down 3 things I feel grateful for. This simple practice has transformed my life. So many Threes get caught up in competing and accomplishing the next big thing. That constant strain and stress can quickly turn into bad habits and diseases for the body. I find that gratitude enables me to maintain that delicate balance between feeling content with who I am (what I have) and embracing the desire for more. Scientific evidence shows that gratitude helps the mind and body in various ways, including lowering blood pressure, stress management, and maintaining homeostasis. As a Three, I want to keep a healthy mind and body so I can keep growing and moving toward my dreams.

Explore spirituality

The topic of spirituality isn't easy, and not everyone is ready for it. But you should know that you don't need to be religious to have a strong spiritual connection. All Threes would benefit significantly from exploring spiritual enlightenment because most of us fall into average and unhealthy levels of expression due to a disconnect with our Higher Self. To find your true self, you'll need to walk that mysterious path of spiritual enlightenment because anything less is just your ego-talk. We struggle with false image, ego fixation, vanity, or wearing too many masks because we're not in touch with our true selves. So we have to perform and make stuff up because that's the only way we know to garner the love we crave deep down.

But once you find your true self and experience unconditional love, your personality morphs into one that doesn't need to fake anything. You learn to be yourself no matter what, and in so doing, you cease to attach your worthiness to accomplishments or external possessions. Dealing with your emotions also becomes easy. The self-image you wear is even more attractive than anything you'd created before the spiritual transformation. It's a lot to take in, so start slowly and consider following spiritual teachers like Deepak Chopra or Neale Donald Walsch, depending on your personal preference.

CHAPTER II

ENNEAGRAM TYPE 4

THE INDIVIDUALIST OR ROMANTIC

I n the following two chapters, we'll cover everything you need to know about the Enneagram Type 4, often referred to as the Romantic or the Individualist. Aptly named, this Enneagram type is most concerned about expressing their individuality and finding their true identity. Similar to the Enneagram Types Two and Three, The Fours are also part of the heart triad. Their core emotion is shame, but unlike the other Types, Fours really embrace and almost drown in this emotion, expressing it more as a sense of deep sadness or melancholy.

Fours believe they are innately different and uniquely talented; therefore, no one can truly understand them or their unique gifts. They are also highly sensitive and acutely aware of their deficiencies. Creativity comes naturally and abundantly to all Fours. When operating at high levels of development, they are plain-spoken, truthful with themselves and others, and possess great emotional depth. These Fours are comfortable being vulnerable and showing who they are unapologetic. This authenticity and intensity is often very attractive. At unhealthy and lower levels of development, however, Fours can be tough to bear, too moody, erratic, full of self-doubt, and inclined to play the victim card as a coping mechanism.

STRENGTHS OF A FOUR

Four are highly sensitive to other people's feelings. They value emotions, and connecting with others emotionally is one of the ways they bond with people. That makes a Four a great listener. People often find comfort and genuine understanding when interacting with this Type.

Fours are also creative and rely heavily on their imagination. Their minds delve into places others are too afraid of or incapable of exploring. That's why some of the greatest artists in human history are type Fours. When a Four finds their artistic expression, they can create endlessly. Each creation is a magnificent performance that enables them to continually find and express who they believe they are.

Another strength you'll find in a Four is how authentic and self-aware they are about their own emotions, strengths, and weaknesses. It gives them the benefit of constant growth and continued learning, which is common among healthy Fours. Unhealthy Fours tend to be hindered by this quality of introspection, causing them to be too self-conscious to the point of paralysis. They may get easily frustrated by their lack or weaknesses, and when they fail, it's harder for them to bounce back.

Key personality traits of Type Four

- Creative
- Authentic
- Compassion

- Passionate

Common hobbies for a Type Four

- Designing
- Photography
- Reading
- Acting
- Listening to music and/or watching movies

FEARS AND WEAKNESSES

Fours have a most complex relationship with their emotions. On the one hand, they aren't afraid to deal with their feelings. Still, they get completely overwhelmed and lost in the melancholy of their unresolved issues. Although they long to be loved and accepted for who they really are, they also believe it's impossible. Talk about emotional chaos. Fours are afraid that they are too flawed and that something is wrong with them or missing, so unconditional love and lasting happiness are impossible. To cope with this fear, they amplify what is different and unique about them, what they can do that others can't. By standing out and pointing out how special they are, they avoid dealing with the real underlying issue, just as we all do.

Another issue Fours experience is this gnawing feeling that no one gets them. They feel misunderstood by others, and in some dark, twisted way, some even assume that they are too "unique" and extraordinary for others to get them. When this thought is entertained by an individual operating at lower levels of development, it can get really destructive to the person's wellbeing and relationships. Unhealthy Fours can become withdrawn, erratic and unbearable because they can't stop feeling sorry for themselves and creating pity parties wherever they go.

It's common to hear statements like, "What I do is so hard and so special, you would never understand me!"

What's the Basic Fear driving this behavior? The fear of being without a unique identity or personal significance.

Fours are idealistic, deeply feeling and sincere people. They are intense and whatever they focus on tends to amplify. Indulging in feelings of inadequacy or that something's missing causes them to become self-absorbed, cynical, passive-aggressive, and at times even manipulative.

How does this basic fear often manifest itself?

Depending on the Four's level of development, there are many forms of expression one might observe in the behavior. For example, it might be overwhelming emotions that manifest as crazy mood swings. It could also be constant jealousy and envy, especially when they see others happy, prosperous, and getting the things they dream about. Another negative expression is manipulating people so they can keep a relationship going in fear of abandonment or comparing themselves to others too much and showing how deficient they are in a particular area. But as I said, it all depends on how developed the Type Four is, so we'll study more about the different levels of development shortly. But first, let's shift focus to the driving desires of a Four.

DESIRES AND MOTIVATIONS

The basic desire for a Type Four is to express their unique individuality and find their true identity. To most Fours, identity is the most important aspect of their entire being. Without a unique identity, life has no meaning for this Enneagram type. So they work tirelessly to find and express this truth about who they really are. Fours are driven to stand out and be spectacular in what they do because they're different. Everyone around them is there "mundane" and unoriginal. They hate people they consider fake and cringe at people who just seem to follow trends. Due to this exaggerated need for authenticity, sticking to their individuality and continuing that personal quest for truth and uniqueness is always at the heart of everything they do.

Core values

As a Type Four, these are some of the core values you may hold dear.

- Originality and creativity
- Authenticity
- Romance
- Beauty, aesthetics
- Imagination
- Self-awareness
- Depth and intensity

Type Four celebrities and famous people you might know include Actress Kate Winslet, Singer Taylor Swift, Writer Edgar Allen Poe, Actress Dakota Fanning, Poet Rumi, Composer, and Pianist Frédéric Chopin, Writer Virginia Wolf, Singer, and Actress Cher, Composer Pytor I. Tchaikovsky, Actor Jonny Depp, Actress Angelina Jolie, Actor Nicholas Cage, Singer Alanis Morrisette, and Singer Song-writer Prince.

Wondering if you could be a Type Four? Here are some personality indicators:

1. As far back as you can remember, you always felt like you were different, even as a little child.
2. You frequently have days where your emotions and thoughts are so loud you can barely focus on the outside world.
3. At your core, you feel that your ability to navigate the deep end of the human experience is a unique gift that you alone have to offer the world - and for that reason, you wouldn't trade it in even if you could.
4. You consider yourself a compassionate and in-tune person.
5. You're incredibly in tune with the thoughts, emotions, and motivations of yourself and those close to you, and it's easy to detect even subtle shifts in other people's moods.
6. The worst thing that can happen to you is feeling nothing or lacking emotion. In fact, you'd rather feel anything than neutral.
7. You hate mundane things, experiences, or people that lack originality.
8. You're always seeking the magical side of everything. More than anything else, you enjoy getting lost in the world of your own vivid imagination.
9. You struggle with envy and feeling that you're always missing out while others have what you want.
10. You're motivated by the pursuit of beauty, originality, and truth.
11. Letting go of the past, especially childhood or painful trauma, is extremely hard for you.
12. You secretly fantasize about meeting someone who understands and loves you so completely that they can, at last, save you from the loneliness and emptiness you've been feeling for so long.

YOUR WINGS

Wings are the numbers adjacent to your Enneagram Type. As a Four, you have-

- The Enneagram Four with Three Wing: "The Aristocrat"
- The Enneagram Four with Five Wing: "The Bohemian"

While you may have tendencies that lean into both wings at various stages of your life, you'll likely be more dominant in one than the other. This will be your most influential and dominant Wing.

Meaning of your Wing

If you're a 4w3 (Four with Three-Wing), you're more enthusiastic, hardworking, and care more about the external world than a classic Four. Your intelligence and creativity are applied in all things, including business and other accomplishments. Operating at healthy levels, the influence of this Wing enables you to become more practical, and it balances out the dreamy, melancholy state with confidence, goal setting, and execution. Unfortunately, average and unhealthy levels could elevate negative traits like envy, competition, and an obsession for validation and appreciation from others.

As a 4w3, you probably want to be in a work environment where your thirst for knowledge and curiosity is quenched. You also want to work with bosses and managers who appreciate and acknowledge all your hard work because that matters to you. Careers best suited to you include but aren't limited to:

- Motivational speaker
- Personal trainer

- Journalist
- Artist (Dancer, Poet, Actor, Painter)
- Graphic Designer
- Interior Designer
- Novelist
- Psychologist
- Career advisor
- Photographer

If you're a 4w5(Four with Five-Wing), you're more self-analyzing, free-spirited, and value your space. Relationships with others and showcasing your skills or motivating others isn't your thing, unlike the 4w3 type. When operating at healthy levels, you're emotionally secure, insightful, intelligent, observant, and fond of understanding people and the world around you. The influence of this Wing at healthy levels is almost like a perfect combination of the heart and head, which makes you very wise and profound. You see beyond what ordinary mortals could. That's why social sciences and arts call to you naturally. That doesn't mean you care about other people's opinions. In fact, you prefer to create things for yourself to fulfill your authentic desires. You enjoy Solitude, and some might even call you a bit eccentric. At average and unhealthy levels, however, the influence of this Wing can cause you to become detached and filled with self-doubt.

As a 4w5, you probably want to be in a work environment where you don't need to have too much people interaction because small talk bores you. You do, however, need an environment where you're free to express your creativity, reflect and seek knowledge and Truth. Careers best suited to you include but aren't limited to:

- Architect
- Actor

- Videographer
- Graphic designer
- Musician
- Librarian

The Arrows and what they mean

Your Enneagram personality type is linked to lines or arrows that show the path of growth or disintegration depending on where you are in life. When moving on a path of disintegration, a Four will fall into the negative trappings of the arrow Two (2), and they'll become more insecure and clingy. This is known as the Direction of Stress or the Direction of Disintegration and typically occurs in the face of pressure or surmounting stress. The other arrow indicates how a healthy version of your personality reacts and grows in more healthy environments. In this case, a Four develops more of the healthier qualities of the arrow One (1), becoming more objective and principled. To understand the concept behind healthy and unhealthy levels, let's go over the various levels of development for a Four.

THE 9 LEVELS OF DEVELOPMENT, FROM LOWEST TO HIGHEST

Levels of Development arise from Riso and Hudson's teachings and the founders of the Enneagram Institute, which is a great place to take your Enneagram Test. Their theory posits that all individuals fall into one of nine levels of functioning. The lowest level is nine, and the highest is level one. The levels are divided into a triad that subcategorizes these levels as healthy (1, 2, 3), average levels (4, 5, 6), and unhealthy levels (7, 8, 9).

Unhealthy Levels

Level 9: This is the lowest and most dangerous level for an adult Four. Typically we are all at this level during infancy. If we fail to rise to higher levels, we experience unhealthy qualities and conditions. For a Type Four, this is where the person feels hopeless, depressed, and highly self-destructive. Some abuse drugs or alcohol to escape, and others have major emotional breakdowns and become suicidal.

Level 8: Although this level is slightly higher than the previous, this Type Four is still stuck in the dark dungeons of their own mind. They are delusional, blameful, highly self-loathing, self-hating, and morbid in their thinking. Everything is tormenting them, and life has no color or beauty. Helping such an individual is challenging, mainly because they try to do everything to drive you away.

Level 7: The Four is a little more productive at this level, but they have difficulty dealing with failure or setbacks. When something goes wrong, they can't handle that sense of shame. It causes them to fall into depression, become alienated from others, and get emotionally paralyzed.

Average Levels

Level 6: At this level, we see a somewhat functional Four, although filled with melancholy, disdain, self-pity, and envy. This Four feels different from others, and they hate seeing others leading a life they presume to be better. While they may wallow in self-pity, they're not really moved to take action to improve what they can't stand about their deficiencies.

Level 5: This Four is moody, hypersensitive, shy, overly self-conscious, and tends to be withdrawn. They are the kind of person that takes every comment, remark, and feedback personally. Emotional outbursts are a common occurrence, and they're not quite in control of their mood swings.

Level 4: At this level, we see a functional individual more capable of being healthy and productive in their world. This Four is artistic, romantic, and obsessed with beauty. They're focused on cultivating an environment around them that's aesthetically beautiful and in tune with their inner fantasies and imagination.

Healthy Levels

Level 3: At this level, the Four is emotionally honest, humane, and true to themselves. They are highly personal and individualistic with a somewhat ironic view of life and themselves.

Level 2: This Type Four is self-aware, introspective, intuitive, gentle, compassionate, and keenly aware of their and other people's emotions. The search for "self" is prominent at this stage of their development, but they do it in healthy, life-giving ways.

Level 1: At this level, the Type Four is at their best. This individual is inspiring to observe, abundantly creative, and they can transform every experience they've ever had into something valuable. They have transcended into their highest expression, and they know their true identity.

ENNEAGRAM FOUR'S PASSION

Type Four's Passion or deadly sin is envy. It typically expresses itself as a sense of lack. Fours have this gnawing feeling that something is missing in them and that others have it, but they were somehow left out. That causes them to look at others we happier, better in some way, and to some extent, even more deserving. Unfortunately, this only creates a sense of inner deficiency, superiority, and inferiority complex.

What the Four needs is equanimity. This is the virtue that will bring much-needed balance, inner peace, wholeness, and healing for the Four. With equanimity, the Four will learn to detach from emotions and stop being controlled by them. They will be grounded in their bodies and recognize that they already have everything they will ever need for a delicious human experience. If you're reading this and realize that you're a Four, this is the work you must do. Bring yourself back to wholeness, back to equanimity.

CHILDHOOD AND EMOTIONAL PATTERNS OF TYPE FOUR

One might wonder, how did the Four develop this belief of lack? Most of the time, it begins in childhood. As children, Fours felt disconnected from both the parental figures in their lives. For some, it was due to extreme reasons like abuse, and for others, it was milder. Regardless of the reasons, Fours felt like their care-givers didn't see them for who they really were.

In many cases, they felt like the advice or comfort offered was too generic and meant for a child totally different from them. This feeling of being unseen and misunderstood within the family unit created a coping mechanism for the Four. They learned to deal with feelings of rejection, isolation, and loneliness by learning to embrace what they felt made them different. More than anything else, a Four just wants to find their identity. As adults, many Fours confess they had fantasies of meeting someone who will really see them for who they are and love them unconditionally– something they've longed for all their lives.

However, to experience that kind of connection requires a certain maturity on the part of the Four, which is why this Enneagram work is vital. The Four must realize that idealizing unconditional love and focusing more on what makes them different isn't beneficial. Instead, they must learn to see where bonds with others can form, which requires conscious effort. The intense, almost uncontrollable emotions that average and unhealthy Fours experience can be transformed through self-awareness and self-acceptance. That's also the path to discovering that nothing is missing. You're not flawed, and you can experience the wholeness you've desired your whole life.

To heal the childhood wound, a Four must reconnect with their Higher Self and recognize that they are worthy. They need to embrace positive feedback and learn to disregard the unhelpful negative emotions that often drown them.

SUBTYPES FOR TYPE FOUR

The Enneagram profiling system allows for 3 subtypes in each type. These are Self-Preservation, Social, and One-to-One (Sexual) variants. Remember, all three instinctual variants exist in all of us. Still, the order in which they stack up determines their influence on our lives. One will be most dominant and the easiest for you to resonate with and observe as behavior and thought patterns in your life. The second will feel a little neutral and less influential, and the third will be the least significant. The third instinct becomes a blind spot for many because it's totally underdeveloped and out of their conscious recognition. Depending on which instinct is most dominant, it will shape your unique personality and how you approach life as a Four.

Self Preservation Four (SP)

Tenacity is the distinct quality of this subtype. It's also the countertype of the Four, so rather than wallow in self-pity, this Four wants to be recognized for being "tough." Even though they are pretty sensitive, they prefer not to complain or share their pain and suffering with others. Instead, they are empathetic and look out for and try to support others. It's easy to mistype this Four as a Type One or Type Seven.

Social Four (SO)

Social Fours are emotionally sensitive and most connected to their suffering. For SO Fours, there's a sense of comfort and familiarity in agony. They enjoy basking in the sweetness of sad poetry and the painful beauty of melancholic music. SO Fours feel everything profoundly and somehow think that their suffering is also what makes them unique and special. Shame is a distinctive quality, and they find comfort in expressing their pain and suffering to others, often attracting support and admiration. The strong emotion of shame triggers plenty of envy and comparison. SO Fours blame themselves for being inadequate and inferior, which only plunges them deeper into shame.

One-to-One/ Sexual Four (SX)

The Sexual Four is intense and has a distinctive quality of competition. They are easy to mistype as an Enneagram Three or an Enneagram Eight because of how demanding, and competitive they tend to be. One-to-One Fours seek to escape their suffering by being the best at what they do and demanding recognition for their work. Surprisingly, these individuals are more shameless than shameful about their personality traits and have no problem getting extremely vocal about their unmet needs. More often than not, the anger or demanding nature of the SX Four is a mask to cover up how sad or confused they really feel.

CHAPTER 12
WORK AND LIFESTYLE TIPS FOR TYPE 4S

As part of your discovery and transformation, it's essential to recognize your triggers, the areas that you struggle with most, and where your opportunities for growth lie.

STRUGGLES OF AN ENNEAGRAM FOUR

Envy

All Fours struggle with feelings of envy in various shades. It stems from that feeling of being deficient or lacking in some way. The average or unhealthy Four feels wholeness, friendship and ease are forever out of reach.

What to do: Take time to notice what you have and the things you've excelled at. Instead of criticizing yourself or comparing yourself with others, acknowledge and focus on the abundance you've got going and let that expand. Practice gratitude and yes, count your blessings. Where your attention goes, energy will flow.

Feeding creativity with pain

Creativity and originality can only come through great suffering for many average and unhealthy Fours. Many believe that they must experience emotional intensity to produce their best work, so they might seek out anguish and grief to channel their creative works. This can be a tormenting experience, not to mention quite destructive.

What to do: Train yourself to realize that creativity is possible even with positive energy. You don't need to dwell on the negative to be the energy. You don't need to stay on the negative to be the creative genius you were born to be.

Finding people who "see you."

When you spend your whole life feeling misunderstood and different, it translates into a life where you just feel invisible and possess a strong desire to connect with someone who can get on your level when it comes to feelings, struggles, and values. That longing creates a terrible existence, and you deserve and can have better.

What to do: Make an effort to connect with people you trust and form genuine bonds. Believe in your ability to attract love into your life. The more you learn to love yourself, the easier it will be for others to appreciate all the long-ignored parts of you. Still, you need to stop idealizing what such a relationship should look like in your imagination.

ENNEAGRAM TYPE FOUR UNDER STRESS

Enneagram Fours are typically stressed when there's too much external pressure. They hate being micro-managed or being forced to follow many rules and guidelines. When their feelings are ignored or if they can't express their true feelings, Fours tend to isolate and brood over their negative emotions and misfortune.

Fours also can't stand being in an environment where they have to put on a happy face when struggling emotionally. Suppose they're working on something and get a creativity block, or there's a lack of progress on their goals. In that case, they'll quickly fall into stress and land on the path of disintegration.

If you're a Four and stress is mounting, don't wait for things to get out of hand. Instead, find someone you trust and just speak it all out. If there's no one to talk to, journal it. Once you've emptied your mind and heart, remember that while emotions are important, they are not always accurate in life. Bring yourself back to the point of recalling your strengths, talents, and what's working. Be in the present moment and engage in some mindfulness practices. Have a set of sticky notes or reminders on your phone for encouragement during this time.

RELATIONSHIPS

Type Fours are deep, novel, and passionate. When it comes to personal and professional relationships, a Four longs to be mirrored, deeply understood, and affirmed by their partner. They spend a great deal of time thinking about their own identity and who they are in the partnership.

In romantic relationships, Fours usually seek partners who will give them the affirmation, love, and understanding that's been missing in their life.

Fours work hard to make the workplace meaningful and special. A leader who is a Four is often authentic, empathetic, creative, expressive, and aesthetically driven. All Fours long to receive appreciation and recognition for the great works they produce at every level of the organization.

RELATIONSHIP TIPS WITH OTHER TYPES

Here are some ways to improve your relationships with other Enneagram Types.

Type 4 & Type 1: The relationship is deep and meaningful with a Type One. You both have a vision of how the world could be. Even though you are opposite in many ways, your energies complement each other well when operating from healthy levels. Type One helps you create some boundaries and get more focused, and you help your partner relax and loosen up a bit. You encourage them to think outside the box and embrace a little creativity.

The main challenge you might face is the internalized criticism and negative self-talk that plagues you, especially if you're at average or unhealthy levels. Your partner can easily get overwhelmed by your emotions, stirring up resentment because they believe you're being improper. On the other hand, you might start to feel like you're constantly critiqued for being different and expressive, and you might lash out when all the One is doing is trying to help you.Grow together by openly communicating your expectations and prioritizing growing to higher levels of development together.

Type 4 & Type 2: You enjoy a deep, emotionally fulfilling relationship with a Type Two. The Two brings a caring, friendly, and warm energy to the relationship. You care about understanding the depth of your partner's heart which helps them become more in tune with their own feelings. The attention you give your partner is also well received. They can pull you out of your inner world and out into the physical world, where you can make real connections with others.

A significant challenge you might face is a communication breakdown, especially since you expect so much from each other but aren't always good at stating it. There are a lot of assumptions, and sometimes those can create blindspots.

Grow together by affirming each other, being more attentive to each other's actual needs, and explicitly stating what you need in the relationship, so there's no room for misunderstandings.

Type 4 & Type 3: With a Three, you'll have a strong, dynamic, high-energy, sensitive relationship. Communication is often transparent and earnest with a Three. They bring a lot of ambition, practicality, and structure to the relationship, and that's good for you. Your self-doubts and negativity tend to take a back seat when with a Three because they are great at bringing out the best of you and cheering you on. Your creativity and emotional depth are great for the Three because it helps them reflect more, slow down, and find deeper meaning in the world.

A significant challenge you might encounter is your different temperaments and how you individually move through life. Sometimes you don't understand each other. Often, the Three finds you emotionally overwhelming and irrational, and you might consider your partner fake or apathetic. They're always moving fast and chasing after something which, at times, you might consider a distraction and something futile that gets in the way of enjoying the beauty of life.

Grow together by setting realistic expectations for one another and notice when tension arises. If you're feeling emotionally neglected, don't allow it to brew into something terrible. Have an open dialogue and find a way to have the experiences you want.

Type 4 & Type 4: With a Type Four, you're essentially in a mirrored relationship that's romantic, thoughtful, passionate, and profound. It's like sharing your life with someone who has the same longing for meaning, beauty, and understanding. You can talk for hours about your deepest thoughts and get lost in your fantasy worlds. You see how things could be perfect and mourn for what's missing.

The main challenge with this relationship is that you both struggle with the same weaknesses. That means you both get moody, you're highly sensitive to rejection, and you experience criticism as a confirmation that you're fatally flawed.

You can grow together by making lifestyle changes and rising to higher levels of development. Incorporate mindfulness practices, journal daily, and practice gratitude. Find enjoyable and healthy ways to stay active together. Become accountability partners and help each other avoid spiraling into negativity when something goes wrong.

Type 4 & Type 5: With a Five, you're in a stable, complex, and comfortable relationship. The Five is well-reasoned and emotion- ally present, bringing a lot of objective wisdom, rationality, and thoughtfulness. You enjoy long conversations and love to explore obscure topics of interest. You empower your partner to become more comfortable with their emotional side and self-expression.

The main challenge you face with a Five is that you both live in your own little worlds, so you need to make an effort to stay grounded in reality. You might also struggle with your partner's constant objectivity and detachment, and the Five might find your emotions overwhelming.

Grow together by appreciating the balance you bring each other. Respect each other's needs and find a way to be together while still giving each other the necessary space.

Type 4 & Type 6: With a Six, the relationship is affectionate, sensitive, and comforting. A Six is loyal and practical, and they can persevere a lot where there is trust. You bring a lot of compassion, emotionality, and self-awareness to the relationship. Your longing to go deeper and discover more helps the Six find more of who they are.

The Six's desire for predictability and steadiness can be difficult for you. You might face a challenge when the Six feels like you're going too far or you're too impractical and unrealistic. That can be deeply wounding for you and may cause you to resent or reject your partner.

Grow together by learning to express your truths in ways that don't wound the other. Ask yourself, "Do I need to express this now? Will it be helpful to us?"

Type 4 & Type 7: With a Seven, you're pretty much the opposite, yet it somehow works because you both enjoy thinking outside the box. The Seven sees all the positive and beautiful things you have, boosting your confidence. And you help the Seven stay a little more grounded and get more comfortable with experiencing all kinds of emotions. There's never a dull or stagnant season in this relationship.

One of the main challenges you might face is when conflicts arise. Your partner likes to avoid any negative emotions, and they might even feel stifled by your need for emotional connection all the time. They might even consider you a killjoy who just wants to keep them down.

Grow together by learning to stay present with each other even when you don't agree rather than escaping or internalizing your emotions. You can also benefit from letting go of the past, especially the things that didn't work out.

Type 4 & Type 8: With an Eight, it's a highly intuitive, intense, and passionate relationship. The Eight offers a sense of protection, strength, and practicality that you crave. There's a magnetic pull between you because you're both on a quest to understand or conquer the mystery in the other. Your sensitivity and emotional vulnerability are something the Eight knows they need. They appreciate how intense you can be in your own way.

A challenge you'll face in this relationship is how reactive, intense and explosive your conflicts and disagreements can be. While it might seem okay, this isn't the healthy version of yourself. Neither of you likes to be controlled. You can't stand feeling misunderstood, so there are likely constant fighting and making up cycles.

Grow together by rising to higher levels of development so you can enjoy your magnetic connection without constantly creating a battlefield. Always start every conflict or disagreement with compassion.

Type 4 & Type 9: You have a sensitive, easy-going deep relationship with a nine. The Nine is non-judgmental and offers you a sense of acceptance that enables you to move toward self-love. Your partner keeps your feet on the ground so-to-speak and allows you to dream. Your energy and creativity are inspiring for your partner. It helps them get more in tune with their emotions and reconnect with the world.

A challenge you might face is during conflicts due to your opposite stress responses. Nines disengage during conflicts because keeping the peace is the only thing that matters to them. You might view this as neglect or not being present, making you more emotionally reactive. That can be overwhelming and unsettling for a Nine.

Grow together by learning to be more thoughtful during conflicts and disagreements. Remember how brutal confrontation is for their personality. Think about your words before using them and allow your partner the space to express their words, too but be kind in this approach.

AFFIRMATIONS FOR ENNEAGRAM TYPE 4

Affirmations can be a great tool when you begin replacing your negative thoughts and habits. Learn to become your own cheer-lead and direct some of that tender loving care inward by speaking words that uplift and encourage you. Here is a list to help you out.

- I heal from my past.
- I appreciate the present moment
- I see beauty and abundance all around me.
- My life is good, and I am grateful.
- I use my experiences to grow.
- I love and accept myself.
- I am whole and abundant.
- I deserve unconditional love.
- I am willing to see others as equals.
- I release myself from overthinking.
- I am willing to make feeling good a priority.
- I am enough.

Remember affirmations only work when what you say and feel are in synch.

DAILY LIFESTYLE TIPS FOR GROWTH AND HAPPINESS

Practice mindfulness

Incorporate mindfulness into your daily routine by finding activities and techniques that help you connect with the present moment. Mindfulness practices enable you to be more non-judgmental, tolerant, and honest with yourself. Consider experimenting with mindfulness meditation or yoga.

Do some volunteer work

Volunteer work is one of the best ways to give back to your community and help people who need and appreciate your help. By pouring your energy into charity, you're putting your energy into the right places. It will be received with deep gratitude. You'll also experience a strong sense of peace knowing that you're doing something meaningful and purposeful.

Cultivate a positive attitude

Adopting a positive mindset doesn't mean faking it. It means keeping an optimistic outlook on life. Notice your inner dialogue and the lens through which you view life. Is it optimistic or pessimistic most of the time? A positive attitude enables you to attract better people and opportunities into your life. It actually allows you to be more gentle and forgiving of yourself when you make mistakes.

Practice self-discipline

Falling into unhealthy habits is super easy for a Four, but as you've learned in this book, spiraling into negativity is not the best way to uncover your true identity and reconnect with your higher self. So I want to encourage you to practice more self-discipline. Refrain from indulging in unhealthy behavior and thought patterns for your growth. You don't need to stop having fun, but you need to eliminate self-destructive behavior. Make this commitment to yourself, and you'll start to see significant shifts internally.

CHAPTER 13

ENNEAGRAM TYPE 5

THE INVESTIGATOR OR OBSERVER

I t's time to uncover the deep mysteries of the Enneagram Type 5, commonly referred to as the Investigator or Observer. Some also like to use the term "quite specialist," and as you read along, you'll soon discover why all these names fit this personality. Fives belong to the thinking center of intelligence or the "head-based" triad. They are the cerebral type, always going with their head and logic. Type Fives are intense, mentally alert, curious, perceptive, secretive, innovative, and prefer to keep to themselves. They are exceptional at focusing on and developing complex skills and ideas. When operating at healthy levels of development, Fives are visionary pioneers, often ahead of their time. They can see the world and universe in ways the rest of humanity can't. That makes them truly extraordinary.

An essential defining quality of a Five is the deep insatiable desire to understand more of the world or the universe. They thirst for knowledge and truth. Many Fives who aren't yet operating at higher and healthier levels of development tend to struggle with detachment and dealing with human interactions or even the daily societal obligations. This can be highly destructive and unhealthy for them and for those engaged with them because they'll come across as absent-minded, aloof, difficult stingy, and eccentric. That's why it's imperative to keep working on personal growth as a Five.

STRENGTHS OF A FIVE

Fives are independent thinkers with a natural knack for thinking through and problem-solving. While other personality types may struggle to understand a complex problem, fives tend to get excited by it. They love challenges and prefer environments where they are free to do whatever it takes to find solutions to a problem.

In fact, fives get bored and easily fall into destructive habits when things aren't challenging enough. Their innovative and inventive nature typically leads them to follow new unchartered grounds and explore concepts yet unknown to society. Type Fives can continually learn and pick up new skills at incredible speeds. That's why many will often become masters at more than a single subject. Another strong quality of a Five is how cool and composed they are, regardless of external conditions. That's mainly due to their natural inclination to focus on problem-solving rather than the emotional charge of any given situation. Other strengths that Fives leverage to their advantage include some of the following:

- The ability to easily cut through complex intellectual ideas and problems
- Creating excellent boundaries for themselves to protect their time and resources
- Maintaining confidentiality and trustworthiness

- Respecting other people's boundaries and space

Key personality traits for a Five

- Curiosity
- Perceptive
- Calm
- Objective and emotionally composed in a crisis
- Insightfulness
- Autonomous and fully independent
- Thoughtful
- Trustworthy
- Often introverted
- Extremely knowledgeable on specific subjects of interests

Common hobbies for a Five

- Working with computers
- Playing board games
- Learning new trivia
- Reading non-fiction
- Participating in solo sports

FEARS AND WEAKNESSES

By now, it's evident that one of the distinguishing expressions of Type Five is the quest for knowledge, truth, and understanding of their world. Fives value time as their most precious resource because it's the one thing they need (that's limited) to achieve their goals. That means they care about doing everything possible to materialize this desire, which indicates that one of their biggest fears is their lack of attainment. For many Fives, anyone or anything that threatens this resource is something they avoid altogether. They easily get overwhelmed when others demand too much from them. Even their own needs can become overwhelming if they feel it's draining too much of their precious resource. Fives tend to withdraw from relationships and maintain a minimalistic lifestyle to focus solely on their intellect and escape worldly demands as a way to cope with this fear.

What's the Basic Fear driving this behavior? The fear of being incompetent, incapable, ignorant, and useless.

Fives get their strength and earn respect for their knowledge and the objective perspectives they offer. In the absence of this, Fives believe they wouldn't get the respect due to them. The fear of being ignorant, helpless, and having their privacy invaded is poignant for a Five. It often expresses itself as withdrawal from people, environments, or situations that conflict with their desires. When some worldly issue demands their attention, they'll try to put them off and deflect those needs and desires as long as possible. In other cases, a Five will get really angry if they are interrupted or pulled from their inner thinking or work. When a demand is made, the first impulse for a Five is to analyze and dissect it as much as possible, aka overthinking. It works when dealing with big problems, but it creates analysis paralysis for everyday stuff.

Depending on their level of development, some of the weaknesses a Type Five might experience include being disconnected from their own feelings, struggling to relate to other people's emotions, and coming off as condescending when interacting with others.

DESIRES AND MOTIVATIONS

The basic desire for a Type Five is to be competent, knowledge-able, and capable. Fives are motivated by the need to possess understanding and knowledge, figure things out and find objective truth. That's why Fives will feel energized and invigorated when learning something new. It can be a new skill, concept, or anything else they haven't learned before. The more challenging it is, the better. They are also happiest when they're discovering something new and when they are by themselves, thinking and reconnecting with their own minds. Of all the Enneagram Types, Fives are the most introverted and analytical. They find great joy in focusing all their energy inward and pursuing knowledge instead of relationships like most other personality types. Because they allocate such little energy toward external demands, Fives take great care to conserve their energy for the things that matter. While that makes relationships with others challenging, the few people they do let in get to experience the richness, stability, and companionship this personality type brings. The Fives also appreciate receiving praise and validation from the few they bring into their world.

CORE VALUES

- Freedom and self-sufficiency
- Knowledge and understanding
- Competency and productivity
- Reputation
- Respect
- Prestige
- Success, achievement, and accomplishment
- Acknowledgment and recognition

Type Five celebrities and famous people you might know to include Billionaire and Microsoft founder Bill Gates, Celebrated scientist and Nobel Prize Winner Albert Einstein, Poet Emily Dickenson, Theoretical Physicist Stephen Hawking, Retired German Politician, and Scientist Angela Merkel, Arthur Stephen King, Geologist, and Biologist Charles Darwin and Dutch Painter Vincent van Gogh.

Wondering if you could be a Type 5? Here are some personality indicators

1. You hate small talk.
2. You see the world and people as things to be gradually understood and won't stop learning until you do.
3. People often underestimate how intense your feelings are since you always seem so calm.
4. You don't open up to people often, but you're fiercely loyal and supportive when you do.
5. You love observing and taking note of every detail in your surroundings.
6. Being self-sufficient and autonomous are non-negotiables in life.
7. Emotions are seldom felt in public and will only be adequately explored in the privacy of your own home. And if it happens in front of someone, you really trust them.
8. You come up with theories about basically everything.
9. You enjoy imagining yourself in the fortress of your own mind, watching your 'avatar' interact with humans.
10. Although life can seem too infinite to truly understand, you know that ultimately, the unexamined life is one not worth loving. And people love you for it.

YOUR WINGS

Wings are the numbers adjacent to your Enneagram Type. As a Five, you have-

- The Enneagram Five with Four Wing: "The Iconoclast"
- The Enneagram Five with Six Wing: "The Problem Solver"

While you may have tendencies that lean into both wings at various stages of your life, you'll likely be more dominant in one than the other. This will be your most influential and Dominant Wing.

Meaning of your Wing

If you're a 5w4 (Five with Four-Wing), you're more of a philosopher who possesses unique beliefs. Your beliefs help you break down your surrounding and societal views. You like to defy the norms, and through the knowledge, you're on a quest to confront the conventional ways. A true innovator at heart, darkness is alluring to you. The unknown is where you enjoy exploring the most, and societal taboos and boundaries mean nothing to you. In fact, half the time, you don't even get why people limit themselves to what's known. Along with your love for dark, hidden, and the unknown sciences, you tend to be more artistic than a classic Five with a Six Wing.

As Five with a Four Wing, you're more in touch with your emotions, giving you more depth than a classic Five, enabling you to be sensitive, reflective, and highly creative. You have the perfect combination of intuition and knowledge when operating at healthy levels. At unhealthy levels, however, the combination of the overly sensitive aspects of the Four Wing and the analytical, detached mind of the Five can lead to a lot of isolation, self-hatred, and contempt for others.

Common career types that best suit a 5w4 include:

- Inventor
- Professor
- Writer
- Artist
- Composer
- Entrepreneur
- Engineering

If you're a 5w6 (Five with a Six-Wing), you're more a troubleshooter than a philosopher. You tend to be more practical disciplined, and organized. Your greatest gift is your ability to use your mind, and you are a little more social than the 5w4. Still, you struggle tremendously with tuning into your feelings or handling stress. You are very observant of the world around you but not particularly introspective. Having the influence of the Six Wing means you can use your analytical mind on practical things that ensure the world will be easier to navigate, more predictable, and maybe even a little safer.

Common career types that best suit a 5w6 include:

- Computer programming
- Accounting
- Law enforcement
- Mathematics
- Engineering

Arrows and what they mean

Your Enneagram personality type is linked to two other "lines" or points worth noting. These lines are called arrows, and each indicates how you show up at your best and worst. One arrow called the Arrow of Disintegration shows the lines of stress (your path of destruction), and for you, that path lies in number 7. As you disintegrate, you pick up the unhealthy habits of an Enneagram Seven and become more scattered, detached, and hyperactive. We'll talk more about stress and how to avoid falling into disintegration in the next chapter.

The other line connected to your Enneagram type is 8, the Arrow of integration. That means that moving on the path of growth and integration, you take on healthy traits from an Eight that make you decisive and more self-confident like a healthy Eight. To understand the relationship between these arrows and how we fall into unhealthy patterns or rise into healthy ones, let's discuss the nine levels of development. The goal is to identify where you might be and move toward the highest level, i.e., healthy level 1.

THE 9 LEVELS OF DEVELOPMENT, FROM LOWEST TO HIGHEST

Levels of Development arise from Riso and Hudson's teachings and the founders of the Enneagram Institute, which is a great place to take your Enneagram Test. Their theory posits that all individuals fall into one of nine levels of functioning. The lowest level is nine, and the highest is level one. The levels are divided into a triad that subcategorizes these levels as healthy (1, 2, 3), average levels (4, 5, 6), and unhealthy levels (7, 8, 9).

Unhealthy

Level 9: As the lowest and darkest level for a Five, we see a deranged, self-destructive adult if they are still stuck at this level. The person is suicidal with psychotic breakdowns, and all they see is oblivion. That's because level Nine is where we begin as infants. For a Five, growing into an adult while stuck at this level of inner growth proves absolutely detrimental for themselves and those around them.

Level 8: At this level, the unhealthy Five is obsessed yet frightened by their own ideas. They are extremely phobic about everything and prey to gross distortions. Everything scares them, and they are pretty hysterical.

Level 7: At this level, the Five is still highly unstable and fearful of aggression. They are nihilistic and eccentric and feel repulsed by others and all social attachments. This person does everything possible to avoid reality.

Average

Level 6: The rise to average levels means that now we're dealing with a person who is cynical, argumentative, radical in their views, and abrasive. They prioritize their inner world and personal vision above all else and can turn pretty antagonistic toward anything that interferes.

Level 5: At this level, we encounter a detached Five who is more preoccupied with their visions and interpretations rather than reality. They are high-strung-intense and still pretty disconnected from the world. Their fascination is more with off-beat esoteric subjects.

Level 4: At this level, the Five is more intellectual and studious and invests a lot of time in model building, preparing, practicing, and gathering more resources. This type of Five loves conceptualizing and fine-tuning things before taking action.

Healthy

Level 3: The rise to this level sees the Five attain skillful mastery of whatever interests them. This individual is excited by knowledge and the quest for truth and understanding. They tend to become an expert in some fields. The Five is inventive, innovative, highly productive, independent, idiosyncratic, and even a little whimsical.

Level 2: At this level, the Five is extraordinarily perceptive and possesses excellent insight. They spend much of their time observing everything and noticing even the tiniest details. Their ability to focus and the insatiable curiosity that engulfs their personality are remarkable.

Level 1: This is the holy grail for a Five, and at this level, we reach the highest and best version of this individual's expression. This Type Five is a visionary. They are open-minded and pioneer discoveries finding entirely new ways of doing and perceiving things.

TYPE FIVE'S PASSION

Fives feel they lack enough inner resources to invest in others, especially for social interaction. They think too much interaction will lead to catastrophic depletion, leading them to withhold themselves from contact with the world. In the Enneagram teaching, this Passion or ego impoverishment is called avarice, although some prefer greed. It simply means that Fives have an insatiable desire for gain or wealth. For a Five, their internal resources and time are the most precious resources they possess if they want to accomplish all their big goals. Unfortunately, too much hoarding of resources and energy out of fear shuts down the heart. It makes it impossible for the Five to receive or give.

What is needed is for the Five to grow and activate the virtue of non-attachment. When this occurs, the Five will become more in sync with the flow of life. They will realize there's no need to hoard anything because life is abundant. There is always enough time, knowledge, energy, and everything they need to complete their mission. The Five will finally be free from the fear that hardens their heart, making them more open-hearted and generous.

CHILDHOOD AND EMOTIONAL PATTERNS OF TYPE FIVE

Fives grew up in an environment that made them feel ambivalent toward their parents. They felt that there was little they did that was wanted or needed by the family. For one reason or another, the Five always felt like an "outsider" looking in rather than nurtured and accepted as one of the group. Sometimes that was because they had abusive or alcoholic parents. Other times, they were the unfavored child, so they felt like the odd duck. In other situations, it could just be that they didn't feel understood or picked up on clues that made them feel a particular way, even if their parents didn't intend it. For instance, certain Fives wanted to feel equal to their parents, so they turned to learning and using their problem-solving skills to master their environments.

Whatever the case, Fives felt they were "odd," so they retreated from the outside world and their families to cope with this loneliness. They spent most of their time hiding in their rooms, looking for a subject they could master or an area of expertise that would allow them to find their place in their family or society. But they always looked for something unique to themselves. So if their siblings were learning to play piano, they would learn to play the cello. They also learned there's a lot of safety, stability, and comfort in being lost in their own mind.

Growing up, Fives become good at expressing either verbally or non-verbally how much they value independence. "Don't ask too much of me, and I won't ask too much of you." Even as adults, Fives hate intrusion, and close physical affection can feel over-whelming and bothersome. They also don't like getting over-whelmed by the thoughts and emotions they experience while spending too much time around people. Thus, even those inter-ested in the people around them prefer to watch and observe from a distance to process their behaviors and understand more about them.

Whether at school or work, Fives need as much time as possible to themselves to devote to mastering their subjects of interest. They are more in their head and identify mainly with their thoughts than emotions.

Average to unhealthy levels, Fives believe that shutting others out and having little to no interaction with the world will lead to happiness.

To heal the childhood wound, the Five must reconnect with their Higher Self and recognize that abundance is the only truth. They need to engage in activities that encourage the mind-body-spirit connection.

SUBTYPES FOR TYPE FIVE

Self-Preservation Five (SP)

SP Five is called "Castle Defender" because this individual is highly protective of their home, personal space, and privacy. This Five has clear and strong boundaries and enjoys living a relatively solitary life with just a few close friends. This Five prefers to observe social life than participate in it. SP Fives are the classic introverts, preferring to reveal very little about their inner world.

Social Five (SO)

SO Five is called "the Professor" and is characterized by a deep insatiable thirst for knowledge and wisdom. This Five loves focusing on big questions, mastering languages and secret symbols of a society or group. A social Five does enjoy connecting with small groups and experts who share their brilliance and high ideal. Still, they are often disconnected from everyday issues and emotions. This Five is more than happy and enthusiastic about sharing values, ideas, and ideals, but they're not too keen on sharing space, time, or inner resources. They also run the risk of being driven by over analysis and overthinking.

Sexual One-to-One Five (SX)

SX Five is called the "Secret Agent" or "Confidant." This one's also the countertype of the group—some of their expressed behavior might come across as counterintuitive for a Five. This individual is cool, analytical, and passionate. Their passion, however, is limited to their life goals and one or two people in an otherwise reserved life. Once they experience "chemistry" with another person, they enjoy the connection, trust, and openness that the relationship fosters. SX Fives risk becoming dependent on the other for that feeling of aliveness and vibrancy, which can lead them to resist sharing that person with others.

CHAPTER 14

WORK AND LIFESTYLE TIPS FOR TYPE 5S

I n this chapter, we'll go over the struggles and stresses that a Type Five may encounter. We'll also cover some strategies to reduce or eliminate stress, and tips for relationship and personal success.

STRUGGLES OF AN ENNEAGRAM FIVE

Emotional unavailability

As a Type Five, you prioritize privacy over everything else. You also know how to disconnect from emotions in real-time. These qualities make it extra challenging to form bonds or experience intimacy in any kind of relationship.

What to do: While you don't need to open up and let in everyone, make an effort to "let in" the few you choose to be in a relationship with. Explore your emotions more openly and at the moment as you feel them, especially when you're with the person you love.

Distractions

All Fives at any level can relate to this because all hate to be interrupted by the outside world. Dealing with the noise of the outside world is often overwhelming and unpleasant. You'd rather pursue ideas and theories in a quiet, safe space void of interruptions, obligations, and people. You need time to tinker with ideas, inventions, art, or other explorations.

What to do: It's okay to protect your space, but I also encourage you to make room for the people you trust. Instead of seeing all people and activities as distractions, see them as investments. Choose the people you will invest in and some activities that you both enjoy, then include that into your strategy as you plan out your life.

Grappling with meaningless purposeless activities

One of the biggest struggles an average and unhealthy Five will experience is a sense of purposelessness and meaninglessness in life. That is especially the case if they allow themselves to turn pessimistic and cynical about the world, people, and the universe. It's hard to see good in the universe when everything around you feels random and absurd.

A Five will have this experience if they don't find an area of mastery and consuming interest, turning them into agitated, stressed-out individuals.

What to do: Find your purpose and bring meaning to everything you do. Pick an area of mastery and keep exploring.

Not having their alone time-respected

As a Five, you're more likely introverted, which means you prefer to be alone more than most people. You also hate small talk and people who barge into your life unannounced. Most people overwhelm you, and it's easy to get overstimulated and irritated when people hijack your time with chatter and socialization.

What to do: Detach healthily. That means you need to carve out time for socialization while still leaving yourself solid unstructured time to just be with yourself daily. Communicate this to your friends and loved ones so they can refrain from barging in and crossing over your boundaries.

Feeling misunderstood

It's common for most Fives to feel misunderstood by family and people in general. Your deep insatiable desire for mastery and competency isn't something many will get. At average and unhealthy levels, this feeling can take a downswing and cause you to feel like what you want to attain is always out of reach.

What to do: If you find yourself feeling that way, work on your inner game so that it doesn't become a weakness that leads you down the path of disintegration.

Facing their darkness and being haunted by it

As a Five, you might notice a peculiar attraction to the darker aspects of life. At healthy levels, this isn't much of a struggle; at average and unhealthy levels, it can turn into an uncontrollable obsession. Some Fives spend a lot of time thinking about the stuff they find most frightening. They might even make a career out of it by studying or creating works of art out of things that scare them.

What to do: While learning how to control and override your fear is a good thing, there is a better and healthier way to deal with the dark side. The higher up your development you go, the easier it will be to face your fears and the dark side healthily.

STRESS AND OPPORTUNITIES FOR GROWTH

Fives often spiral down into unhealthy thinking and behavior patterns when stress mounts. If they're unable to connect with their inner world, a lack of clarity kicks in, causing them to be hazy. When this is left unchecked, the Five will develop traits of an unhealthy Seven. They might behave recklessly, become impulsive and find unhealthy ways to distract them from their stress as a way to shut down "thinking."

What stresses out a Five?

- Feeling like life is meaningless and without purpose
- Physical malnutrition and neglect
- Not finding an area of expertise to master
- Feeling incompetent or incapable
- Becoming dependent on others
- Having their time or privacy invaded
- Extreme isolation and lack of connection
- Not getting enough alone time

Opportunities for growth and ways to avoid disintegration

- Engage in activities that enable you to reconnect with your body and your emotions. Experiment with yoga, playing an instrument, creative writing, or whatever idea excites you as long as it engages your emotions and brings you close to understanding your physical and emotional side.
- Prioritize time outside connecting with nature or make some time for socializing with others.
- Read books and watch videos on emotional intelligence, then find a few people to practice these skills with.

- Prioritize your health by developing a healthy eating lifestyle and regularly working out.

RELATIONSHIPS

As a Five, you take a more intellectual and objective approach to everything. In relationships, that curious, investigative and independent nature is attractive, but it can also create problems if you're not making an effort to express intimacy and open up with loved ones.

RELATIONSHIP TIPS WITH OTHER TYPES

Type 5 & Type 1: With a One, you're in a stable, dependable relationship where each partner respects boundaries and structure. The One brings curiosity, independence, hard work, high standards, ethics, and mutual interests. You bring that sense of self-sufficiency, independence, steadiness, and a judgment-free environment that gives your partner great comfort.

A challenge you might encounter in this relationship comes down to values. Ones believe in objectivity, but they hold fast to their convictions once they find the truth. On the other hand, you are very open-minded and flexible, so your truths can evolve as you learn more. This "rigidity" with your partner is often frustrating, and you tend to appear "unpredictable." Your partner's constant advice and help can also feel more like criticism because you're sensitive to feedback, which might cause you to withdraw. However, that only makes the Type One feel insecure about the relationship. Grow together by appreciating differing perspectives and validating each other's viewpoints. You should also remind each other frequently that you're there for each other, especially when you don't see eye to eye.

Type 5 & Type 2: With a Two, you're in a loyal, nurturing, warm and comfortable relationship. The Two brings your feelings to the foreground and enables you to be more grounded in the present moment. Your commitment, trustworthiness, wisdom, and competence are highly desirable for a Two. Remembering even the tiniest details about your partner makes them feel special and loved.

A challenge you might find with your partner is your emotional temperament and how you respond to stress and conflict. Twos are naturally passionate and expressive, while you are always calm and rational. This might leave your partner feeling like you're disengaged and detached. On the other hand, you might feel overwhelmed by all that emotion or as though your partner is too intrusive. It's essential to work through these differences and find healthy ways to deal with stress and misunderstandings. Grow together by recognizing that your needs are not at odds despite your differences. Remind your partner that you're not abandoning or rejecting them when you seem detached.

Type 5 & Type 3: With a Three, the relationship is dynamic, full of energy, stable, and filled with creativity. Your partner brings confidence, high energy, and sociability, and you admire their expertise and accomplishments. The Three admires your creativity, depth, objectivity, and thoughtfulness. You stabilize your partner, and they help take you out of your shell.

A challenge you might encounter is how you both move through life. Threes are fast and tend to think on their feet. You're more steady and prefer to conserve your energy. That can sometimes brew frustration, creating a tug-of-war as you pull in opposite directions. Grow together by getting in touch with your feelings and openly communicating expectations. Choose to learn from each other and leverage each other's strengths.

Type 5 & Type 4: With a Four, the relationship is deep, meaningful, and full of new explorations. You both enjoy indulging in lengthy conversations on topics of interest. The Four is emotionally present and imaginative and enables you to become more comfortable with your emotions and self-expression. You help the Four become more rational and thoughtful about their ideas and actions. It helps to keep your partner grounded and stable.

A common challenge occurs when the Four become frustrated with your detachment and objectivity. They might feel that you're not present or understanding of their emotions. You might become overwhelmed by the emotions of a Four, especially when they fall into average or unhealthy levels. Grow together by respecting and openly communicating each other's needs.

Type 5 & Type 5: With a fellow Type Five, the relationship is stable, founded on a deep respect for each other's privacy, and enriched by the thirst you both have for knowledge. Having a partner who truly gets you and values the same things you value can be extremely comforting.

A challenge you will face in this relationship is how you both withdraw when things get challenging. Because you both love space and privacy, you can easily get complacent, and things may just naturally fall apart due to mutual neglect. Although you deal with conflict calmly, objectively, and rationally, it might be tough to have an emotional connection and, in turn, real intimacy. Grow together by reaching out and connecting emotionally at a human level. It's okay to exert some social and emotional energy, so put a little more effort into this.

Type 5 & Type 6: With a Six, you have a balanced, secure relationship that allows both of you to be yourselves without the fear of getting overwhelmed. The Six brings thoughtfulness, loyalty, and attentiveness. They enjoy how careful and thoughtful you are with your words, actions, and approach to life. Your partner enables you to stay more connected and become less isolated.

A challenge you might face with this relationship might be how you approach problems and situations. The Six trusts in rules and procedures more than their own thoughts, and you are an out-of-the-box thinker who only trusts in your own intellect. That can create a lot of frustration for both of you. So, grow together by embracing each other's differences and dedicate time each week to do something you both enjoy and like to learn about. Practice working through little differences often so that, when big issues show up, you can move through those without picking each other apart.

Type 5 & Type 7: With a Seven as your partner, life is an exciting adventure with more to discover daily. Your relationship is whimsical, and there's never a dull moment. The Seven brings spontaneity, freshness, and even a little bit of a rebellious streak. You enjoy having someone bursting with curiosity to explore the world together. You also help your partner become a little more grounded and serious in their pursuits.

You may encounter a challenge with this relationship when you're both stressed. When stress hits, you withdraw and choose to conserve your energy by becoming undemanding and focusing on things that matter. Your partner goes in the opposite direction and becomes more demanding, expending more energy and chasing yet another new thing. That can lead to significant misunderstandings. Grow together by having an open dialogue about how you'll manage stressful situations together and incorporate both your strengths.

Type 5 & Type 8: With an Eight as a partner, you find something you need in them and vice versa. Your partner helps you become more in tune with your intuition and power. They get you focused on being more practical and tending to your needs. You help the Eight become more aware of their impact on others and the importance of slowing down every now and then. The relationship is deep, self-assured, loyal, and rich with thought-provoking conversation.

A challenge you might encounter regularly is what happens when that good debate becomes too intense or what happens when conflict arises. You both hate being anything but self reliant. Vulnerability doesn't come easy, so there's a natural tendency for communication and connection to break down. Grow together by making an effort to ensure you don't drive a wedge between you. Work on finding a deep emotional connection and admit your own needs. Be vulnerable together and protect that safe space.

Type 5 & Type 9: With a Nine as your partner, the relationship is comforting and stable, and they just accept you as you are for all that you are. Your partner brings ease, kindness, and patience into the relationship, and you enable the Nine to reconnect with their inner childlike curiosity. The relationship allows for self-awareness, peace, and autonomy.

A challenge you might encounter is that your partner may become passive-aggressive and stubborn when conflicts arise. Your rational and objective approach tends to make your partner feel distanced. Still, because they prefer to avoid conflicts at all costs, they might not say anything, which may create resentment. Grow together by keeping an open dialogue at all times, especially during disagreements. Give each other time and space to process your thoughts and feelings but always have the conversation to air things out. You should also find ways to stay grounded and present by doing something you enjoy.

AFFIRMATIONS FOR ENNEAGRAM TYPE 5

- I am present and mindful
- I make peace with uncertainty
- My life has great meaning and purpose, and I am living it
- I support others lovingly
- I feel secure knowing what is needed, and I trust that I will receive what I need
- I practice being in flow and tapping into the generosity of the universe because life is abundant

Remember affirmations only work is what you say, and feel are in alignment.

DAILY LIFESTYLE TIPS FOR GROWTH AND HAPPINESS

Find your purpose. This won't happen instantly, but with a bit of self-discovery, you can uncover the purpose that lights up your life.

Practice mindfulness daily

Find a practice that resonates with you. Think of this as an exploration or an experiment and test yoga, meditation, pilates, journaling, gratitude, or simply taking long walks daily. Whatever enables you to come into the present moment and reconnect mind-body-spirit is what you need for growth and happiness.

Make time to tune into your emotions

This one will feel like a challenge at first because it's easy to shelf emotions or not deal with them, so here are two ways you can work on this. The first is to journal how you feel at the end of each day. The second is to pause when you experience that emotion and then do the STOP method. STOP means: **S**top; **T**ake three deep breaths; **O**bserve your breath and your body; **P**roceed from this new calm state. As you observe your body, notice the emotion and how you're experiencing it, then just release it. Allow it to flow like water flowing downstream.

Make time for the relationships that matter to you. And if you don't have any relationship, it's time to allow one into your life. I'm not saying you meet the world, but I am encouraging you to reach out to someone you feel you can trust and allow that bond to form over time.

CHAPTER 15

ENNEAGRAM TYPE 6

THE LOYALIST OR SKEPTIC

The loyalist, sometimes referred to as the skeptic, is one of the more interesting paradigms in the Enneagram teachings. They tend to be complex and intriguing. It's often easy to mistype them for other personality types because of their character complexities. Loyalists are witty, practical, and always think about everything that could go wrong in any given situation. The title skeptic is quite apt because this personality type has serious trust issues and constantly doubts everything, including their own thoughts. They have difficulty trusting anyone, so they always need reassurance from the few they deem authoritative. Inherent in their personality is a tendency to be anxious and nervous about everything. But I suppose that makes sense given their need to consider worst-case scenarios at every new turn.

Loyalists belong to the head triad of thinking center alongside Fives and Sevens. They need to feel safe and attempt to do so through meaningful relationships. Safety and security are of primary importance to Sixes, so most of their decisions are rooted in the need to be in a safe space with people they can trust.

STRENGTHS OF A SIX

Loyalists are inquisitive and always curious to learn new things. They're great problem solvers and highly perceptive. Sixes tend to be great strategic thinkers. They are organized and well-liked because they have a certain warmth to them.

Another strength of a Six is their trustworthiness and the warmth they bring to their relationships.

Key personality traits for a Six

- Committed
- Problem solver
- Trustworthy
- Responsible
- Detail-oriented and precise
- Excellent team player

Common hobbies for a Type Six

- Volunteering
- Writing fiction
- Reading
- List-making
- Listening to music

FEARS AND WEAKNESSES

Sixes fear that things will go wrong in their life. No matter where they are or what's happening, Sixes want security so bad and fear not having the support and guidance they need to the point where they trust no one. On the one hand, they crave safety, support, and reassurance, but on the other, they don't trust anyone, including themselves, to provide it when it matters. So they're constantly seeking to close this gap by looking for some external authoritative power.

What's the Basic Fear driving this behavior? The fear of being unsupported and lacking proper guidance.

This fear shows in behavior as constant anxiety and overplanning to prepare for the worst. The brain of a Six is on constant over-drive, ever thinking and rethinking plans to find all possible solutions.

DESIRES AND MOTIVATIONS

The primary desire of a Six is to be supported and feel secure. That's why loyalists surround themselves with people they feel will support them unconditionally. In turn, the Six is also extremely loyal and trustworthy. While it may seem a little needy because they need constant reassurance and support, the Sixes make wonderful friends and companions.

Core values

- Commitment
- Trust
- Security
- Reliability

Type Six celebrities and famous people you might know include author Mark Twain, Actress and model Marylin Monroe, Director and producer Woody Allen, Actress Jennifer Aniston, Actress Julia

Roberts, Comedian Ellen Degeneres, Actor Tom Hanks, and former U.S. Presidents George H.W. Bush and Richard Nixon.

Wondering if you could be a Type Six? Here are some personality indicators:

1. You need a lot of reassurance with almost everything you do.
2. You're critical of yourself because you constantly worry you've let others down.
3. You hang on to relationships/friendships for much longer than you should.
4. Decision making is a daunting task because you see an infinite number of options.
5. You fear being abandoned by others and left alone.
6. You thrive on stability and predictability.
7. You're good at deciphering between logic and emotion.

YOUR WINGS

Wings are the number adjacent to your Enneagram Type. As a Six, you have -

- The Enneagram Six with Five-Wing: "The Defender"
- The Enneagram Six with Seven Wing: "The Buddy"

While you may have tendencies that lean into both wings at various stages of your life, you'll likely be more dominant in one than the other. This will be your most influential and dominant Wing.

Meaning of your Wing

If you're a 6w5 (Six with a Five-Wing), you're more independent, analytical, and more interested in pursuing solitary hobbies than communal ones. Sixes with this Wing find they have a greater need for time alone whether they can concentrate on the things they need to solve, whether personal or professional. They like to work in fixed systems like academics or analytical jobs where the rules are well established, and a predictable path is clearly outlined.

As a 6w5, you're also great at taking care of your family and serving others, doing things the right way, and ensuring those loyal to you are happy.

You're incredibly reliable, responsible, intellectual, and excellent at problem-solving. Careers best suited to you include but aren't limited to:

- Banker
- Web developer
- Paralegal
- Professor
- Business consultant
- Financial analyst

If you're a 6w7 (Six with a Seven-Wing), you're much more extro-verted and playful than the Six with a Five-Wing. The influence of the Seven Wing enables you to be more easy-going and adventur-ous. You're willing to take on a bit more risk, and you're not afraid to fail and make mistakes as you grow. Although you're still cautious, you tend to approach the world more light-heartedly. Sixes with this Wing are more empathetic and connected to others. There's a strong desire to create bonds and relationships they can depend on, making their relationships enriching and dynamic. Unfortunately, this makes them less independent than the 6w5; however, this social need only increases their self-confidence and fuels their energy at healthy levels.

You're energetic, a great team player, and quite social at work. Careers best suited to you include but aren't limited to:

- New anchor
- Real estate agent
- Professor
- Nurse
- Actor
- Author
- Sales representative

The Arrows and what they mean

Your Enneagram personality type is linked to lines or arrows that show the path of growth or disintegration depending on where you are in life. When moving on a path of disintegration, a Six will fall into the negative trappings of the arrow Three (3), and they'll become competitive and arrogant. This is known as the Direction of Stress or the Direction of Disintegration and typically occurs in the face of pressure or surmounting stress. The other arrow indicates how a healthy version of your personality reacts and grows in more healthy environments. In this case, a Six develops more of the healthier qualities of the arrow Nine(9), becoming more relaxed and optimistic. To understand the concept behind healthy and unhealthy levels, let's go over the various levels of development for a Six.

THE 9 LEVELS OF DEVELOPMENT, FROM LOWEST TO HIGHEST

Levels of Development arise from Riso and Hudson's teachings and the founders of the Enneagram Institute, which is a great place to take your Enneagram Test. Their theory posits that all individuals fall into one of nine levels of functioning. The lowest level is nine, and the highest is level one. The levels are divided into a triad that subcategorizes these levels as healthy (1,2,3), average levels (4,5,6), and unhealthy levels (7,8,9).

Unhealthy

Level 9: This is the most dangerous level for any human being. It's rock bottom for a Six, especially if they are adults going through life at this level. The adult Six at this level is hysterical, self-destructive, and seeks any means (even suicide) to escape punishment. They tend to cope by turning to alcoholism and drug abuse.

Level 8: Still pretty unhealthy, this Six is violent, fearful, and completely irrational. They feel persecuted and that others are out to get them. Unfortunately, they're stuck in a self-manufactured torture cycle where what they fear becomes their experience.

Level 7: The Six are fearful about their safety and security at this level. They are panicky, volatile, and feel powerless. Such a person typically seeks out a stronger authority or belief to act as their safety net. They also criticize everyone who isn't part of their safe zone.

Average

Level 6: As the Six rises to average levels of operations, we see the person compensating for the internal turmoil and insecurities. They blame everyone for their problems and mistrust everything and everyone except those they look up to for security. This person may come across as authoritarian while being fearful of authority, and they often use fear to silence others.

Level 5: At this level, the person is indecisive, cautious, ambivalent, anxious, and tends to give mixed signals. The internal confusion makes them react unpredictably.

Level 4: This Six invests all their time and energy into whatever they believe will keep them safe and create stability in their life. At this level, the Six is constantly overthinking and overanalyzing everything. They are more organized and structured. They anticipate problems at every turn and find comfort in their alliances.

Healthy

Level 3: This is the beginning of the journey to the highest and best version of an Enneagram Six. This individual is a community builder. They are responsible, reliable, trustworthy, and hardworking and invest their energy doing work that helps others.

Level 2: At this level, the Six can inspire others and makes a great leader. They are affectionate, lovable, and form strong bonds with others.

Level 1: This is the highest and best level for a Six. The individual is self-affirming, independent yet symbiotically interdependent, and cooperative at this level. They have great courage, optimism, and love for serving others—a true inspiration for everyone in their world.

ENNEAGRAM SIX'S PASSION

The Six's Passion of deadly sin is Angst or anxiety. It typically expresses itself as the subconscious need to protect yourself from everything happening around you. Sixes tend to spin out of control mentally as they worry about everything that could go wrong.

What the Six needs is courage. This is the virtue that will bring back your power and reassurance that you can handle life and whatever challenges lie ahead. It will enable you to see that the only absolute security you can have is the one you create for yourself and that power exists within you.

If you're reading this and recognize that you're a Six, this is the work you must do. Bring yourself back to wholeness, back to courage.

CHILDHOOD AND EMOTIONAL PATTERNS FOR ENNEAGRAM SIX

You might be wondering how the Six developed this anxiety and where the ego fixation came from. As children, Sixes felt their environment was too unpredictable and dangerous. Even though they had a protective figure, the protection they received also experienced constant threats for whatever reason. That could be because the protector was abusive at times, or maybe they struggled with addiction or mental health issues, making them highly volatile. It could also be that the protector was too strict with illogical and over-the-top punishment whenever the child made a mistake. Regardless of the root cause, the child learned to depend on protection from the caregiver, who at times betrayed the very essence of security that the child believed in. That caused the child to develop the habit of constant analysis to prepare for any unpleasant situations. It also conditioned the child to view themselves as powerless.

In adulthood, this conditioning leads to an adult who constantly seeks that exact protective and authoritative figure because they aren't used to being their own source of security. At the same time, they tend to be skeptical of everything and everyone - always hoping for the best but expecting the worst.

Sixes feel separated from their internal guidance. They are plagued by the need to find the right course of action and be around their "people," making them very divisive. The constant doubt and anxiety are detrimental to their success in life and can only be eliminated through growth and inner work.

To heal the childhood wound, a Six must walk the path of self-empowerment and self-love. They need to learn to depend on the safety and security of their Higher Self instead of relying on others.

SUBTYPES FOR ENNEAGRAM TYPE SIX

The Enneagram profiling system allows for three subtypes in each type. These are Self-Preservation, Social, and One-to-One (Sexual) variants. Remember, all three instinctual variants exist in all of us, but the order in which they stack up determines their influence on our lives. One will be most dominant and the easiest for you to resonate with and observe as behavior and thought patterns in your life. The second will feel a little neutral and less influential, and the third will be the least significant. The third instinct becomes a blind spot for many because it's underdeveloped and out of their conscious recognition. Depending on which instinct is most dominant, it will shape your unique personality and how you approach life as a Six.

Self Preservation Six (SP)

For this subtype, warmth is the essential quality that stands out. Although they are the most fearful and insecure of the subtypes, SP Sixes are also warm-hearted in their interactions with others.

They repress their anger and tend to be overly cautious with everything because they never want to make mistakes or disappoint others. They focus on building strong familial alliances as a coping mechanism to create a strong fort for themselves and those they love.

Social Six (SO)

SO Sixes are dutiful. It's easy to mistype them for Enneagram One because of their strong moral compass and tendency to see things are black and white. These individuals are rational and prefer to follow the rules and do things the right way.

One-to-One/Sexual Six (SX)

As the countertype of the subtype Sixes, SX Sixes are intimidating. They come across as bold, assertive, and a little rebellious. It's easy to mistype them for Enneagram Eight because they always run in the direction of their fears as a way to counteract their anxiety. Because the Sixes naturally mistrust people, SX Sixes will seek out concrete and pragmatic ideologies because they feel more truthful and grounded.

CHAPTER 16

WORK AND LIFESTYLE TIPS FOR TYPE 6S

B efore we discuss how you can improve yourself on this quest of self-discovery, we must explore some of the struggles you may experience on your journey. For some of you, the struggles already dominate your life, and if that's the case, you'll find the suggestions offered pretty helpful.

STRUGGLES OF AN ENNEAGRAM SIX

The love-hate relationship with authority

By this, I mean you love the security that comes with looking to others for authority, but at the same time, you're skeptical about people who call themselves authority. People who seem self-assured and confident that their way is the only right way seem "too good to be true ."That's probably why you start playing the devil's advocate as soon as you find someone you like.

What to do: The only real solution to the issue of security and authority comes down to trusting your inner guidance. I know that's a tall order, but that's why you're reading this book, isn't it?

The battle with uncertainty

Is there anything you don't doubt? The lower you are in your development, the higher and more overwhelming your doubts become. On the outside, people see a charming, good-humored, or even self-assured person, but you know the truth. Deep down, you live in a constantly shaky world. You're scared of abandonment, rejection, deception, betrayal, death, and everything that lies in between. You worry that you'll screw up your relationships, job, or assigned project. It's a hard battle, and you face it daily. While other Enneagram types might succeed in distracting themselves from their fears, your fear seems to live face-to-face with you.

What to do: The only way to overcome fear is to find your Higher Self and live from that strength and fundamental Truth. Work on developing to higher levels in your spiritual connection. The more you work on your mind and spirit, the more grounded you'll become, and fear will no longer stand in your way.

Perfectionism and rigidity

Often as a Six, you might feel like you can only relax and feel secure once all your problems are solved. In other words, you'll be happy and at ease when X happens (X is the thing you're working on or worried about). You might also struggle with perfectionism, especially in your relationships. That could be because you tend to be overly critical to avoid making mistakes or disappointing the people you care about. Both these issues are rooted in the same false belief, and it's because of that unceasing anxiety that you become so rigid in your behavior.

What to do: Recognize and quantify how much time goes into worrying and catastrophizing everything. Notice how much time this takes away from being happy, present, and effective in your daily life. Incorporate some mindfulness practices, so you can learn to accept yourself and silence the mental chatter that robs you.

You don't trust yourself

As a child, you may have deliberately or unintentionally received the conditioning that you shouldn't trust your instincts. As a result, you spend most of your time looking to teachers, mentors, coaches, and institutions to tell you what's right. Unfortunately, giving away that much power erodes your ability to become all you were born to be. It creates a breeding ground for mistrust. If you can't trust yourself first, you can never truly trust anyone else because Truth is always unknown to you.

What to do: Invest in anything and everything that enables you to cultivate a healthy and unshakeable self-belief. This should not be an ego-based belief but rather a Higher Self belief. You will know absolute freedom when you learn to trust in that voice above and beyond what others say, no matter how authoritative they might be.

ENNEAGRAM TYPE 6 UNDER STRESS

Sixes are typically stressed when they feel unsafe or there's a disorder in their environment. They also cannot stand disorder in their environment, corruption, lack of structure or clarity, and wishy-washy behavior from others.

When stress is more than they can handle, Sixes naturally disintegrate into the arrow 3, meaning they pick up unhealthy behaviors from Enneagram Three. That causes them to ignore their values and focus on covering up their insecurities, fear of rejection, failure, and abandonment. They might even become super boastful about their accomplishments, especially around the people they want to impress. Suppose they are stressed because they're not feeling the reassurance and support needed from their group or an authoritative figure. In that case, they might become overly self-absorbed and arrogant, playing the devil's advocate. All of which are rooted in the internal stress and mounting fears they're attempting to conceal.

If you're a Six and you're wondering how to deal with burnout or the fear of chaos and uncertainty, here are a few things you can do:

When the idea of the worst-case scenario hijacks your mind, instead of succumbing to that fear, play it out like a movie in your head. Ask yourself, "if that bad thing happens, then what?" Keep asking yourself that question until you either prove that you're not going to die out of this situation, and your brain will naturally give in to a more calm and optimistic state. You'll find calm and solid ground by realistically assessing the situation.

You can also consider playing the simple game "what if I'm wrong and the opposite thing happens?" By asking this question, you give your brain permission to consider the opposite (the positive) aspects of things. This is a simple yet powerful game for Sixes because often, the brain leaps into the worst-case scenarios for everything.

RELATIONSHIPS

Sixes are thoughtful and protective of those they love. They make great partners, especially when operating at healthy levels of development. If, however, the Six isn't well developed in their self-mastery, they do struggle with trust. That makes the relationship challenging because they can be considered controlling and too skeptical.

As a Six, you know all too well how hard it can be to trust someone, especially a romantic partner. Consistency, commitment, responsibility, and devotion matter to you, so your right partner needs to bring a certain level of compassion, kindness, and trustworthiness to your relationship. They need to be transparent for things to work well.

Below are tips on cultivating a healthy, loving relationship with other types and what you might expect. If none of the suggestions resonate, that's okay. This is to raise your curiosity and awareness of your strengths and weaknesses in relationships.

RELATIONSHIP TIPS WITH OTHER TYPES

Type 6 & Type 1: With a One, you have a relationship you can count on because you're both committed, responsible, and value loyalty. You and your partner are dutiful and want to make the world better. The One grounds you and creates a safety net that soothes your skepticism. Your wittiness helps the One lighten up, and you're able to see various possible outcomes to any scenario, which can be helpful for the Enneagram One, who tends to be rigid in their choices.

Although the Enneagram One's self-assuredness and decisiveness can inspire you to cultivate the same qualities leading to an enriching relationship, you may encounter a challenge when your partner becomes resentful or overly critical of you. That could make you reactive and anxious, making you appear hypocritical to your partner. Sixes and Ones are very uncomfortable with conflict, leading to the blame game. Grow together by keeping open communication and leaning into your fun side. Find ways to be spontaneous together and not take each other's missteps too seriously.

Type 6 & Type 2: With a Two, you're in a supportive, warm, attentive relationship. Your connection is built on friendship and responsibility. The Two brings empathy, affection, and comfort, making you feel that your partner always has your back. Your desire for steadiness offers the Two a sense of feeling prioritized and valued.

A challenge you might face in this relationship is your ambivalence. The tendency to test your partner by pulling them close and then pushing them away only amplifies insecurity for your partner. The Two might go into "fix it" mode, trying to help you win back your love. Unfortunately, that might make you feel like they are too controlling.

Grow together by finding time to continue growing your friendship and connection. Both of you need to verbalize your needs and how you can meet those needs. Don't play the assumption game in your relationship.

Type 6 & Type 3: With a Three, the relationship is dynamic, dutiful, responsible, and resilient. You trust each other and make a great team. The Three brings ambition, a great work ethic, encouragement, and optimism that inspires you to pursue your passions. You keep your partner grounded and help them slow down a little more.

A challenge you might face in this relationship comes down to your values. As a Six, you might struggle with the shape-shifting nature of a Three, causing you to have trust issues. The Threes hard-driving "always on" energy can also conflict with your cautious and more conservative nature. That can cause the Three to feel like you're holding them back.

Grow together by validating each other's focus of attention and staying present in the relationship. Have an open dialogue about your emotions, and make sure you work through the minor issues that could create cracks in the relationship.

Type 6 & Type 4: With a Four, you've got a deep relationship. The Four always wants to go emotionally deeper, and your commitment to the relationship facilitates that level of expressiveness and exploration. The Four brings compassion and self-awareness, and you're practical, loyal, and sensitive. You have plenty of similarities, and that can be pretty comforting.

A challenge you might face here is that you're extremely practical while your partner tends to be driven by their passions. That can create conflict, especially when you don't see eye to eye on something. The Four might also struggle with the fact that you want everything to be predictable with strict boundaries, and they don't like being boxed in or limited in life. Grow together by handling your conflicts better. Recognize that sometimes, your partner's pursuit of authenticity may not align with your need for consistency. And that's okay. Work through these experiences and be thoughtful in your responses. Ask yourself, "do I need to express this right now? Will it be helpful to our relationship?"

Type 6 & Type 5: With a Five, you have a deep relationship that allows you to be yourself without fear of judgment or overwhelm. Your thoughtfulness, loyalty, attentiveness, and balance enable the Five to stay more connected and less isolated from the world. The Five's steadiness, stability, cautious approach, and trustworthiness appeal to you.

A challenge you might face in this relationship is when it comes to decision-making. Your tendency to trust existing rules and procedures can be frustrating for your partner because Fives trust their intellect more than other people's opinions. While you're both analytical in your approaches, when you don't see eye to eye, things can become pretty messy because you may start picking apart the relationship instead of focusing on the issue at hand.

Grow together by learning to step back from a heated situation and giving each other some space to realign internally, then come back and work through the differences compassionately. Find something your both enjoy and like to learn about and dedicate time to that activity each week.

Type 6 & Type 6: Being in a mirrored relationship is easy and comfortable, and it's like having a best friend who just gets you. Establishing the deep trust necessary for a lasting partnership can take time because you're both Sixes, but nothing can separate you once you find it. You can relax, have fun together, and know that you've got each other's backs. There's no guesswork about where you stand in the relationship.

A challenge you'll face is how you deal with conflict. You may say things in the heat of the moment that you don't mean, which may crack the trust you've worked so hard to build. Grow together by expressing compassion regularly and step back from the heat of the moment to avoid saying things you'll regret later.

Type 6 & Type 7: You're in a fun-loving relationship with a seven. You're kindred souls who play off one another's strengths. The Seven brings adventure, light-heartedness, and fun to the relationship, and you offer stability, balance, and light caution, which enables the Seven to get grounded.

 A challenge you might face in this relationship is that you both struggle deeply with anxiety, fear, and insecurities. But the way you cope with them differs significantly. You create structure, stability, and systems to deal with your anxiety and fears, whereas Seven copes by constantly looking for external distractions and things that spark their energy. Your partner can quickly get tired of your pessimism and desire to be free of the rules and "silly" considerations that you hold dear. Be respectful of each other's ways and find that middle ground where you can agree. Grow together by recognizing that both your perspectives in life carry significant value.

Type 6 & Type 8: With an Eight, you're in a protective, dependable relationship. You compliment each other well. The Eight brings clarity, decisiveness, and transparency, enabling you to trust them. Your warmth and kindness make the Eight feel embraced and cared for.

A challenge you might face here is that you're both reactive in conflicts, and when things go wrong, you don't feel like you can trust each other. You might find the Eight's bullish approach a little off-putting, and your partner sees your concerns and questioning as a lack of trust. If you're counterphobic, conflicts may become explosive as neither party will back down easily. Grow together by developing your self-control and recognizing that you're both work in progress. Being vulnerable is a tough call for both of you, and that's okay. Support each other and offer reassurance because you're both looking for safety, not control. Remind each other that you're in this together.

Type 6 & Type 9: With a Nine, you're in a supportive, affectionate, and loyal relationship with many shared values. You share a mutual devotion and comfort. The Nine brings kindness, acceptance, and stability to the relationship. Your action-oriented nature can help the Nine become more active in their own life.

A challenge you might face is during stressful periods because the Nine tends to withdraw, which can feel like abandonment. Your emotional reactivity can also be detrimental because the Nine likes to avoid all conflict and prefers to tip-toe around things which may also feel like they are not being transparent. Grow together by supporting each other in voicing your needs and wants. Figure out what you really want in a relationship and encourage your partner to do the same, then openly share this vision so you can move toward it together.

AFFIRMATIONS

- I am safe in this present moment
- I am willing to trust more
- I know my worth
- I am compassionate with others and myself
- I choose to see the best in others

Remember affirmations only work when what you say and feel are in synch. Only use affirmations you deeply resonate with.

DAILY LIFESTYLE TIPS FOR GROWTH AND HAPPINESS

- Work on your self-talk. Mental chatter is one of the leading causes of the high stress and health issues you might experience. The more you work on your mindset and train your brain to maintain healthy, loving self-talk, the easier it will be to keep calm. Consider learning how to meditate. It's one of the best ways to calm a worrying mind and elevate your physiological state.
- Invest some time daily to decompress and tune into your body. Use deep breathing techniques to bring a sense of calm throughout your body.
- Learn to let go of non-essential responsibilities that overwhelm you. There's nothing wrong with letting

others take over a project. Recognize when you're simply taking on too much and just say no.

- Move your body daily. Exercising is a great way to increase stress-reducing endorphins in the brain. Find exercises you enjoy and work up a sweat daily or at least three times a week.

CHAPTER 17

ENNEAGRAM TYPE 7

THE ENTHUSIAST OR ADVENTURER

T he Enthusiast or Adventurer is the Enneagram Type Seven. This personality is best known for their carefree, adventurous behavior. They are bubbly and bursting with energy. In this chapter and the next, we'll dig deeper into the personality, fears, desires, strengths, struggles, and ways to reconnect with your higher self while increasing happiness in your life.

The Enneagram Seven is an idealist and visionary. They are energetic, charismatic, creative, and love taking risks. A Seven is a big picture thinker and prefers to live outside the box of conventional advice. Most Sevens are multi-talented and passionate about various things. They have a genuine concern for human growth and progress while at the same time having little regard for social status or etiquette.

Sevens have a strong desire to learn more about themselves and discover new things. They can be pretty impulsive and abstract in their communication, but they are great storytellers. Sevens love to animate everything they say and constantly seek the good in life and others. In fact, they tend to struggle to deal with anything in themselves or others that aren't positive. But more on that later.

Enneagram Seven is part of the head triad or thinking center, making them witty and intellectual. Like Fives and Sixes, they are very observant of their environment and use their creative imagination to make decisions. However, the main difference is that, unlike the Fives and Sixes, who are very grounded and careful with their choices, Sevens tend to be more impulsive with their decisions and actions.

STRENGTHS OF A SEVEN

One of the greatest strengths of an enthusiast is their belief in the positive aspects of life and people. They are good finders in the truest strengths of the word, always encouraging, uplifting, and cheering others to pursue their dreams.

Sevens are great at seeing the big picture in almost everything. They have an agile mind that can switch between multiple things quickly. If you're with a Seven, things are always dynamic and fun because they know how to brighten the mood and uplift everyone around them.

Another strength is that Sevens never take themselves too seriously. That enables them to bounce back quickly in the face of a setback or failure.

Key personality traits of a Seven

- Versatile
- Curious
- Bold
- Playful
- Energetic

- Cheerful
- Resilient

Common hobbies for type Seven

- Podcasting
- Stand-up comedy
- Adrenaline inducing activities
- Trying new foods

FEARS AND WEAKNESSES

Sevens fear missing out on the good life or getting trapped and stuck in a rut. That's because of the core fear of being deprived or experiencing pain. They constantly seek exciting, novel, and fun experiences to cope with this fear.

The idea of limitations and restrictions is very unappealing to a Seven. Unfortunately, this can lead to behaviors like escapism, impatience, avoidance, and overindulgence, especially when the individual isn't operating at healthy levels.

What's the Basic Fear driving this behavior? The fear of being trapped in pain or lacking something.

This fear can manifest itself in constant busyness, which brings with it fatigue. It also shows up as a lack of follow-through and withdrawing from commitments without notice. But the Seven would rather put up with exhaustion than deal with mundane experiences or pain.

Some Sevens go on the opposite extreme and excessively plan their fun adventures. This over-enthusiasm and constant need for movement and entertainment is also an unhealthy manifestation of the same core fear.

DESIRES AND MOTIVATION

As pleasure-seeking personalities, all Sevens have a fundamental desire to be stress-free, happy, and satisfied. Sevens are motivated by the desire to have their needs fulfilled. If faced with dull, boring, or scary experiences, Sevens do everything possible to retreat from that environment. They typically go to great lengths to find happiness and excitement. When operating at average or unhealthy levels, the Seven will jump from one exciting thing to another, chasing after the next big high.

Core values

- Fun
- Pleasure
- Optimism
- Flexibility

Type Seven celebrities and famous people you might know include singer and songwriter Elton John, entrepreneur Richard Branson, Singer Katy Perry, actress Elizabeth Taylor, Comedian Eddie Murphy, President John F. Kennedy, Actor Jack Black, and Robin Williams.

Wondering if you could be a Type Seven? Here are some personality indicators:

1. It's easy for you to pick up new skills, but you don't put much into mastering any of them.
2. You quickly feel depressed if you're resources are limited in any way. You're happiest when you can experience and achieve whatever you want.
3. Most of the time, you find the present pretty dull.

4. Despite your seemingly carefree attitude, you know exactly what you want out of life and won't stop till you get it.
5. Your enthusiasm level mirrors that of a five-year-old regardless of your actual age.
6. Patience isn't something you handle well because you want everything you've planned to happen a.s.a.p
7. FOMO is real and alive!
8. You can't stand people who say, "Be realistic."
9. You're passionate and obsessed with the future and its possibilities. In fact, you spend most of your time thinking about and planning the future.

YOUR WINGS

Wings are the number adjacent to your Enneagram Type. As a Seven, you have -

- The Enneagram Seven with Six-Wing: "The Entertainer"
- The Enneagram Seven with Eight-Wing: "The Realist"

While you may have tendencies that lean into both wings at various stages of your life, you'll likely be more dominant in one than the other. This will be your most influential and dominant Wing.

Meaning of your Wing

If you're a 7w6 (Seven with a Six-Wing), the influence of this Wing makes you more focused and responsible. Your spontaneity and the need to be steady, secure, and focused make you the most sociable personality type across the Enneagram system. You also become more disciplined, productive, and organized with greater foresight.

At work, you'll get along with practically everyone. You're charming, funny, adult, and childlike at the same time and, at times, a little cheeky. People love working and being around you. They also feel they can rely on you. Some of the best careers you can go for include but aren't limited to:

- Photographer
- Journalist
- Media planner
- Travel agent
- Tour Guide
- Publicist
- Travel writer

If you're a 7w8 (Seven with an Eight-Wing), the influence of this Wing makes you more assertive and driven. You're not as concerned with relationships as the 7w6 because your focus is on creating your own experiences and winning in life. If you fancy material success and power, your willpower is strong enough to get you there. However, you'll need to be mindful not to fall into unhealthy habits like workaholism, power games, and overstimulation that tend to be the downfall of an Enneagram 8. Living on the edge of life is excellent but make sure you're operating at high levels of development which we'll discuss shortly.

Careers best suited to you include:

- TV anchor
- Sales manager
- Promoter
- Travel agent
- Motivational speaker
- Firefighter

- Paramedic
- Travel writer

The Arrows and what they mean

Your Enneagram personality type is linked to lines or arrows that show the path of growth or disintegration depending on where you are in life. When moving on a path of disintegration, a Seven will fall into the negative trappings of the arrow One (1), and they'll become more self-critical and perfectionistic. This is known as the Direction of Stress or the Direction of Disintegration and typically occurs in the face of pressure or surmounting stress. The other arrow indicates how a healthy version of your personality reacts and grows in more healthy environments. In this case, a Seven develops more of the healthier qualities of the arrow Five (5), becoming more focused and curious about life. To understand the concept behind healthy and unhealthy levels, let's go over the various levels of development for a Seven.

THE 9 LEVELS OF DEVELOPMENT, FROM LOWEST TO HIGHEST

Levels of Development arise from Riso and Hudson's teachings and the founders of the Enneagram Institute, which is a great place to take your Enneagram Test. Their theory posits that all individuals fall into one of nine levels of functioning. The lowest level is nine, and the highest is level one. The levels are divided into a triad that subcategorizes these levels as healthy (1,2,3), average levels (4,5,6), and unhealthy levels (7,8,9).

Unhealthy

Level 9: At this level, the Seven is at their lowest and most destructive state as an adult. This is where the person is completely burned out, panic-stricken, depressed, and in deep despair. They lose their health and energy, and some become suicidal or addicted to drugs. It's pretty common to overdose at this stage of their life because they are entirely out of control.

Level 8: At this level, the person is still out of control, erratic and compulsive in their behavior. They have massive mood swings and feel like they'll never fully understand life or get what they want. This person can't get grounded or stabilize their emotions.

Level 7: This Enneagram Seven is narcissistic, flashy, and exuberant. They jump from place to place and person to person, desperate to quell their insurmountable anxiety. Many tend to cope through drugs and other addictive behaviors.

Average

Level 6: The rise to this level does bring some relief, but the Seven is still struggling with addiction. They engage in a slew of constant activities, trying to seek the next "high" through adventure and new projects. As an adrenaline junkie, this Seven doesn't know when to stop and lacks follow-through in whatever task they start. They come across as pushy, demanding, jaded and insensitive.

Level 5: This Seven is constantly busy because they fear being bored. They are great storytellers, flamboyant, and always have tons of ideas. Unfortunately, they're still not grounded or focused enough to complete what they start making them unreliable. Unable to discriminate what they need, this person tends to exaggerate and overindulge in almost everything.

Level 4: At this level, the person is future-oriented and almost always excited about some new plan. They always want to have more options and choices available to them, and they enjoy keeping up with the latest trends in society. This person is adventurous and worldly-wise.

Healthy

Level 3: At this level, the Seven is stepping into the path of integration, becoming a more practical, productive, and reliable individual. They can channel their multi-talents in prolific ways and quickly become accomplished achievers who generally do many things well.

Level 2: At this level, we encounter a Seven who is inspiring and contagious because of their high positive energy and enthusiasm. This individual is reliable and eager to learn, and they've finally learned to be grounded while still enjoying their adventurous spirit.

Level 1: The holy grail for an Enneagram Seven is where the individual rises to their best version becoming spiritually reunited. That, in turn, raises their curiosity, thirst for knowledge, and new experiences while simultaneously being grounded and grateful in the present. They develop more depth in life and become joyfully awed by the simple wonders of life. Better still, they find their perfect work-life balance while still making time for new adventures.

ENNEAGRAM SEVEN'S PASSION

The Seven's Passion or deadly sin is gluttony. It typically expresses itself as overindulgence in life and the pursuit of more. Sevens tend to jump from one experience to another, always seeking to taste a little bit of everything.

What the Seven needs is sobriety. That's the virtue that will get you in touch with your true Self and the present moment. By coming to the deeper part of the Self, you become more grounded in the moment, less distracted, and fearful of boredom or unpleasant emotions. You realize that you can enjoy life fully and have it all without overindulging.

If you're reading this and recognize that you're a Seven, that's the work you must do. Bring yourself back to wholeness, back to sobriety.

CHILDHOOD AND EMOTIONAL PATTERNS FOR ENNEAGRAM SEVEN

One might wonder how the Seven developed this reckless, care-free, gluttonous quality. The ego fixation can be traced back to childhood when the disconnect took place thanks to what's referred to as "nurturing deficiency." As children, Sevens experienced neglect resulting in a lack of bond with the supposed caregiver. Whether that was because the primary caregiver was abusive, struggling with addiction, or having mental health issues, the child developed a deep sense of emptiness. Sevens filled that loneliness with distractions, activities, objects, and possibilities that would excite their senses and keep them busy. They chased after anything and everything they thought would make them happy because they felt that would compensate for the nurture they always felt was out of reach.

As adults, the same emotional patterns play out as excessive optimism, constant adventure, and chasing after whatever they believe will keep them stimulated and happy. Unfortunately, they don't know how to deal with long-standing issues or even face uncomfortable situations. Sevens fear being alone or being hurt and sometimes walk away from projects or a relationship purely because they're afraid of being disappointed.

To heal the childhood wound, a Seven must reconnect with their Higher Self and learn to receive love, care, and affection from others. They need to enjoy the present moment and prioritize creating meaningful relationships.

SUBTYPES FOR ENNEAGRAM TYPE SEVEN

The Enneagram profiling system allows for 3 subtypes in each type. These are Self-Preservation, Social, and One-to-One (Sexual) variants. Remember, all three instinctual variants exist in all of us, but the order in which they stack up determines their influence on our lives. One will be most dominant and the easiest for you to resonate with and observe as behavior and thought patterns in your life. The second will feel a little neutral and less influential, and the third will be the least significant. The third instinct becomes a blind spot for many because it's underdeveloped and out of their conscious recognition. Depending on which instinct is most dominant, it will shape your unique personality and how you approach life as a Seven.

Self Preservation Seven (SP)

The SP Seven is a masterful networker and connector, always looking to build a strong "family" of people they can leverage to fuel their adventure-seeking prowess. These individuals love the good things in life, and everyone in their world plays a vital role in meeting their needs. These are the kinds of people who brag about how they have friends all over that they can call on at any time. They're good at getting what they want and are perhaps the most practical and rational of the three subtypes.

Social Seven (SO)

As the countertype for the subtype, Sacrifice is the key quality for the Social Seven. They act against their gluttony by being of service to create a better world. It's easy to mistype this SO Seven with an Enneagram 2 because they are warm and often put the needs of others (or a group they support) ahead of their own. The fun-loving, adventurous spirit is still alive, but they tend to direct their energy toward a mission of helping everyone enjoy life more.

One-to-One/Sexual Seven (SX)

With the SX Seven, the key quality is fascination. This Seven experiences life through rose-colored lenses. They have a contagious enthusiasm and optimism and only see good in all people and all things. SX Sevens believe that life is a fantasy novel, and they are very good at helping those they're interested in "fit into the magical costume" the Seven creates for them. In other words, SX Sevens know how to make others feel special, and that attracts a lot of interest. Unfortunately, getting swept away into the charm, intensity, and sparkles of a Seven can lead to heartache because their attention is typically temporary. As soon as they find a new object of attention, they immediately disappear, which can be deeply shocking to the person interacting with a Seven. One more thing to note is that SX Sevens cannot stand anything they consider dull and dreary and often walk away from overly predictable relationships.

CHAPTER 18

WORK AND LIFESTYLE TIPS FOR TYPE 7S

As part of your discovery and transformation, it's essential to recognize your triggers, the areas that you struggle with most, and where your opportunities for growth lie.

STRUGGLES OF AN ENNEAGRAM 7

Getting bored

You get bored most of the time because you're mismanaging your energy and focus. However, this boredom is rooted in deficiency at average and unhealthy levels and typically leads to very unhealthy actions. Almost all Sevens will struggle with this because the truth is, even the healthy ones need that sense of adventure and challenge in their life.

What to do: Study your boredom. How soon after you get bored do you seek out distractions? What emotions lie in your boredom? What does that feel like in your body? What memories does your boredom bring up? Is there pain associated with it that you're trying to avoid? Journal whatever revelations you get. Writing down what you really feel can help you become more self-aware and heal some of those hidden wounds. Again, it won't be easy, but it will change your life.

Feeling trapped

Freedom is one of the core values and the basic desire for a Seven. The world is an endless treasure trove of activities and experiences, so commitments can make you feel like a bird trapped in a cage. Even if you crave marriage, long work contracts, and family commitments, these things also give you tremendous anxiety.

What to do: Open your mind to the possibility that commitment, discipline, and freedom can go hand in hand. Relationships and work opportunities can last a long time but still facilitate the sense of novelty and adventure you crave. Seek out these types of engagements.

Feeling distracted and unfocused

It's easy for average and unhealthy Sevens to be invaded by too many ideas and possibilities. Many complain of feeling out of control and even overwhelmed. Then focusing does become an arduous task.

What to do: Meditation is a great way to help your mind calm down. It also enables you to practice being in the present moment, strengthening your focus. Find meditation practices that excite you and turn them into a daily ritual.

No follow-through

This behavior is often rooted in a lack of focus and discipline. When a Seven gets distracted or bored, they tend to abandon what they were doing and find something new to excite them.

What to do: Cultivate discipline in your life. It won't be easy, but you must do it. If you can train your brain to stick with something to completion, it will change your life and improve your professional perception.

ENNEAGRAM TYPE SEVEN UNDER STRESS

Sevens tend to get really stressed when they're micro-managed, bored, or when they feel like they don't have enough personal freedom. They also don't like being cooped up for too long or stuck in the same place. Other things that stress Sevens significantly include financial problems because they can't do and have everything they want. They also don't like being stuck in detail work or doing nitty-gritty stuff because they're big picture thinkers. Suppose you give a Seven too much responsibility or rigid deadlines. In that case, they can easily fall into high-stress levels, which may, over time, cause them to disintegrate into the unhealthy habits of an Enneagram One. That's quite alarming for everyone around this individual because they go from a carefree, fun-loving, and optimistic person to a rigid control freak. They can become overly critical and bury themselves in work or projects to take their mind off their struggles.

If you're a Seven and wondering how to deal with high-stress levels, consider meditation and other mindfulness practices. These will bring you into the present moment and calm you down. You can also use music to help you mirror your emotions. Once you determine which emotions are creating this unpleasant feeling, don't run and hide. Instead, find healthy ways to process those emotions. Journaling your feelings is a great way to release them. Realize that both positive and negative emotions are essential for the full human experience.

RELATIONSHIPS

Type Sevens are fun, enthusiastic, energetic, and spontaneous. When it comes to personal and professional relationships, a Seven never wants to feel caged or restricted.

In romantic relationships, Fours usually seek partners who will enable them to feel connected and grounded without being stifled.

Sevens work hard to make the workplace fun and exciting. They enjoy new events, sharing their creative ideas, and boosting morale, but they need support to remain accountable and follow through on their assignments.

RELATIONSHIP TIPS WITH OTHER TYPES

Here are some ways to improve your relationships with other Enneagram Types.

Type 7 & Type 1: With a One, you're in a case of "opposites attract," which can be profoundly fulfilling if both operate at healthy levels. In many ways, you complement each other because you bring curiosity, reliability, and hard work into the relationship dynamic. The One helps you become more steady and conscientious, and you help them see the little ways that everyday life can be worth celebrating.

A challenge you might face in this relationship is the feeling of being trapped in the boredom of routine, strict rules, and predictability that your partner adores. Meanwhile, your partner might feel like the "adult" in the relationship.

Grow together by developing higher levels of awareness so you can appreciate the balance the other brings.

Type 7 & Type 2: With a Two, the relationship is warm, nurturing, spontaneous, and fun. The Two bring generosity, concern for the welfare of others, and loving attention and dedication to your needs. You inspire them to dream bigger and think outside the box. In this relationship, the Two show you that it's okay to think beyond your personal needs.

A challenge you might face is the difference in perspectives regarding emotional connection. The Two might feel that you're not present enough, especially when feelings arise. That will cause your partner to respond by either demanding that you understand their needs or trying to "fix" you. Regardless, this doesn't end well because it causes you to feel trapped in the relationship. Grow together by learning to talk through conflicts rather than staying positive and avoiding tough talks. Reassure each other of your commitment and when you have these unpleasant talks, reward yourselves with something fun.

Type 7 & Type 3: With a Three, the relationship is adventurous and gregarious, and you play off each other's strengths. There's never a dull moment here. The Three is ambitious, focused, poised, and sensitive to the relationship. You're relaxed, courageous, and resilient, and you know how to keep things interesting, which makes you super attractive.

A challenge you might face since you're both constantly doing things and keeping busy is that you may avoid dealing with feelings and conflicts. Your partner may also feel embarrassed by your naturally boisterous nature and the tendency to say whatever comes to your mind. Meanwhile, you might get frustrated by the Three's constant desire for productivity and work. Grow together by sharing feelings. Be open and yes, it will be uncomfortable but do it anyway. Learn to slow down every once in a while and just enjoy being in each other's company.

Type 7 & Type 4: With a Four, you're in a colorful, emotionally expressive relationship. The Four helps you stay grounded and creates a safe space to explore your emotions. You help your partner see all the wonderful positive things in life, which helps boost their confidence. Although you're opposite in many ways, you both tend to think outside the box, and you're constantly intrigued and fascinated by each other's way of life.

A challenge you might face in this relationship is how you handle conflict. Given your varying reactions to emotions and conflict, your partner may feel like you don't care about them or respect their feelings. Meanwhile, the constant need for emotional exploration and connection could feel a bit stifling to you, and at times your partner might feel like a killjoy who just wants to keep you down. Grow together by practicing a lot more present moment mindfulness. Instead of escaping or internalizing disappointment or unpleasant moments, talk it out and let things go. When things don't go as planned, learn to be okay with that.

Type 7 & Type 5: With a Five, you're in a thoughtful relationship with constant learning, investigation, and deep diving into hobbies and things of interest. The Five brings knowledge and curiosity that you find highly appealing. Your spontaneity is quite refreshing for your partner and gets them out of their head so they can enjoy life a little more.

A challenge you might face is how opposite you are when stress hits. You like to run into the future without care. The Five is more conservative and self-reliant. While you both want to meet your own needs, the way you approach them is very different and often leads to misunderstandings. Grow together by openly communicating your needs and leveraging each other's strengths. The combination of knowledge and intrigue can work in your favor as long as you take the time to integrate this into the relationship.

Type 7 and Type 6: With a Six, you're stable, predictable relationship, and you enjoy playing off one another's strengths. The Six brings stability, caution, and pragmatism that you appreciate, and your fun, adventurous spirit lightens their careful disposition. Your partner appreciates the fact that you've got their back.

A challenge you might face in this relationship is that you both struggle deeply with anxiety, fear, and insecurities. But the way you cope with them differs greatly. You get bored quickly, and your partner's structure and pessimistic outlook might become frustrating. Meanwhile, the Six might see your carefree attitude as too unstable and untrustworthy, creating cracks in your relationship. Grow together by recognizing that both your perspectives in life carry significant value. Be respectful of each other's ways and find that middle ground where you can both agree.

Type 7 & Type 7: With a Seven, you're in a mirrored relationship where you understand each other's need for independence. You ride the waves of fun and possibility, the relationship is light-hearted and full of energy, and you're constantly bouncing ideas off one another. You can enjoy a resilient, deeply loving, thriving, and joyous connection.

You might face a challenge in this relationship when conflict or adverse events arise. Your natural impulse is to avoid all unpleasant experiences. You might also have difficulty finding common ground on what you want out of the relationship and life. Grow together by being more intentional about the relationship. You should also prioritize downtime together and connect emotionally at a deeper level, especially when conflicts arise.

Type 7 & Type 8: With an Eight, the relationship is captivating, dynamic, and intense. The Eight keeps you grounded in reality, attentive to practical matters, and focused. You help your partner lighten up a little and have more fun in life.

A challenge you might face is that you quickly get frustrated when you don't get what you want. Eights need to feel in control and have things their way, so when you go off on your own, that might get a little intense. Your cheerful disposition may also come across as inauthentic, and when an Eight is around people they consider inauthentic, they tend to be more self-protective. Because you're both strong-willed, your relationship can quickly tune into a battle for autonomy. Grow together by slowing down long enough to notice your emotional reactions and ask yourself if these reactions are constructive. Be present with your emotions and learn to process them in healthier ways.

Type 7 & Type 9: With a Nine, the relationship is calm, steady, and flexible. The Nine offers a very reassuring calmness as it makes you feel accepted and loved just as you are. You bring a sense of fun and aliveness that helps the Nine break out of their shell and try new things.

A common challenge you might face is due to your stubbornness, especially when things aren't going well. You're more likely to be the first to surface conflict since you hate feeling trapped by negative emotions. Unfortunately, your tendency to move past conflicts too quickly may cause your partner to feel trampled. Nines take time to process things, and when they're not encouraged to speak their Truth, they tend to withdraw and become passive aggressive. Grow together by learning to work through conflict together. Have those tough conversations with compassion. After a successful unpleasant conversation, reward yourself with something fun. It's also a great idea to remind each other that conflict will not jeopardize the relationship.

AFFIRMATIONS

- I am satisfied and grateful for every experience
- Every obstacle is just a learning opportunity
- I choose to be happy and content
- I am willing to trust the timing of my life
- I can slow down and still have fun

DAILY LIFESTYLE TIPS FOR GROWTH AND HAPPINESS

Avoid stimulants

Addiction is a common issue with Sevens, so I want to encourage you to avoid using any stimulants as much as possible. Besides, you already have boundless energy. Do you really need 5 cups of coffee? Instead of more coffee or other addictive substances, find ways to raise your feel-good hormones even more, either through daily exercise or giving yourself healthy treats like a spa day each week.

Learn some deep breathing techniques.

Deep breathing techniques are a great way to process emotions. You can find YouTube videos from various teachers with numerous techniques to apply. Just stick with the teacher you best resonate with.

Confide in a friend you trust

When boredom, distractions, and negative emotions kick in, instead of avoiding them, talk to a trusted friend or a coach so they can support you and keep you accountable, especially if you're working on an important project.

Spend time practicing stillness and just being in the present moment

Find daily practices of solitude, whether through sitting alone with some soothing music, journaling, or walking in nature. Learn to fall in love with yourself and enjoy being in your company. Your path to healing starts with solitude.

CHAPTER 19

ENNEAGRAM TYPE 8

THE CHALLENGER OR PROTECTOR

The following two chapters cover everything you need to know about the Enneagram Type 8, often referred to as the challenger or the protector. Similar to Nines and Ones, Eights make up the Body triad of the gut center of intelligence. Aptly named, this Enneagram type is self-assured, assertive, and loves to be in charge. Eights are most concerned with protecting themselves and those under their care. They don't like authorities that impose ideologies or regulations on them, so they're constantly looking to lead the group/family/company. That means they have trouble processing and dealing with feelings of anger. But unlike the Nines and Ones, Enneagram Eights don't repress or hide their anger. If anything, they use it to their advantage as an intimidation technique.

Eights believe they must always be in control of everything. Their primary focus is to control the situation internally and externally in personal or professional settings. That makes vulnerability one of the peeves for an Eight. Letting their guard down and allowing themselves to be influenced by someone they trust is tough, but it can happen with maturity and a lot of inner work. Eights are unapologetic in their demeanor and communication. They are straight shooters who sometimes come across as arrogant and insensitive. One thing you can depend on is that an Eight will always be honest, direct, and straight to the point, and they expect the same from others.

STRENGTHS OF TYPE EIGHT

One of the strengths an Eight possesses is finding that balance between indulging in the things they love and nurturing the people they care about. Eights can relax and unwind when it's time to do so.

Resourcefulness is also a strength you find with the Eight because they know how to leverage what they have to get what they want. If there's something they need but lack, Eights are excellent at forming allies to leverage other people's resources.

Another great thing about Eights is how bold and courageous they are. They love to stand up for the underdogs and the little guys in their world and aren't afraid to use their power to protect the weak. That behavior is rooted in the mindset that the world is unjust and weak people are at a disadvantage. So the strong must defend the defenseless.

Key personality traits of an Eight

- Self-confident
- Resourceful
- Assertive
- Decisive

- Strong
- Domineering

Common hobbies for an Eight

- Public speaking
- Debating
- Exercising
- Extreme sports

FEARS AND WEAKNESSES

The primary fear of Type Eight is being controlled or harmed by others. This individual sees vulnerability as a weakness that could lead to powerlessness, loss of control, and getting hurt. Type Eight will attempt to remedy this fear by avoiding all situations that may cause them to feel vulnerable or powerless.

For most Eights, the issue becomes complex because they deny their fears and weaknesses. Because they don't want to admit that they're afraid to lower their guard, their relationships tend to be pretty rocky, especially with those they love the most. At average and unhealthy levels, their intensity and passion for life and goals can be overwhelming and intimidating to others. Control and domination may turn dark, and they might mix their need for justice with revenge. Because power is a focal point for an Eight, they must be mindful of how they acquire and utilize the power they crave. Used well, an Eight's power can do a lot of good but used poorly, it can bring a lot of heartache and devastation to others. Many people interacting with average or unhealthy Eights also describe a lack of respect and too much confrontation from the Eight.

What's the Basic Fear driving this behavior? The fear of being controlled and harmed by others.

Type Eights believe that you are what you do. Somewhere along their life journey, they were conditioned to believe that the world is a tough place where only the strong survive. So they decided to be among the survivors by taking the lead and always striving to be in charge so they could keep their power.

How does this basic fear often manifest itself?

This fear is expressed in behavior as being too pushy, domineering, and even ego-centric. The person may come across as aggressive, confrontational, rude, impolite, and intense. In some cases, especially the very unhealthy Eights, they are notorious for creating drama around them, making it difficult to have real connections with anyone.

DESIRES AND MOTIVATIONS

The basic desire for a Type Eight is independence. They want to protect themselves and remain in control of their own lives. Being self-governed and in charge is their primary aim for a Type Eight, and nothing should jeopardize that. That typically makes an Eight incredibly courageous, strong, and dependable.

Enneagram Eights march to the beat of their own drum, unfettered by external sources' demands and perceived obligations. Once they feel secure about their actions and plans, they attack head-on with force and willpower until they get the job done.

They also love nurturing the people they care about, although they do it authoritatively. As challengers, they aren't afraid to impose their ideas and wills on others. While it tends to work out well for everyone under their care, things can get heated pretty quickly if you're on the opposing side of type Eight.

Core values

- Power
- Influence
- Achievement
- Perseverance
- Strength

Type Eight celebrities and famous people you might know to include minister Martin Luther King, Jr., Billionaire and former President Donald Trump, author Ernest Hemmingway, Comedian, and actor Jack Black, Singer Franck Sinatra, actor Sean Penn, Actress Susan Sarandon, actor Alec Baldwin, singer Aretha Franklin, Former U.K Prime Minister Winston Churchill, and President Franklin D. Roosevelt.

Wondering if you could be a Type Eight? Here are some personality indicators

1. When you're up against a problem, your first instinct is to tackle it single-handedly and head-on. Asking for help doesn't even cross your mind.
2. You refuse to enable self-pity or self-sabotage in the people you love. You want to see your loved ones thrive, even if that means you have to be the one who doles out some tough love.
3. You're not one to bend over backward trying to please people. You are fair and just in your decision-making, but you also know you can't make everyone happy all the time.

4. It's essential to have firm boundaries within your relationships. That way, you still feel as though you'd be in control of every other aspect of your life should the relationship end.

5. Often, your attitude comes off as intimidation or abrasive to others. But you know the world absolutely needs people like you, and in that crisis, you're the first person everyone would want by their side.

YOUR WINGS

Wings are the numbers adjacent to your Enneagram Type. As a Type Eight, you have-

- Enneagram Eight with a Seven-Wing: "The Maverick"
- Enneagram Eight with a Nine-Wing: "The Bear"

While you may have tendencies that lean into both wings at various stages of your life, you'll likely be more dominant in one than the other. This will be your most influential and dominant Wing.

Meaning of your Wing

If you're an 8w7 (Eight with Seven-Wing), you're more extro-verted than the Eight with a Nine-Wing. The combination of Seven's fun, outgoing and impulsive personality combined with your natural assertiveness and energy makes you quite the super-nova of every. It also means you're less guarded and more eager to enjoy life. Of course, the downside to this powerful combination is that 8W7 can quickly turn into an oppressive, uncaring, cruel maniac who thinks themselves omnipotent when operating at unhealthy levels. But on the other hand, a mature and highly developed individual will be the opposite, with great strength, vitality, and compassion. Basically unstoppable. Such individuals can have a lasting, sometimes legendary impact.

As an 8W7, you likely want to be in an entrepreneurial environment. Whether you work for yourself or the board of directors, it's essential that you are in charge and leading the rest of the people. You're most fulfilled when you can create optimistic and innovative plans, share your thoughts and opinions openly, and go after big things. Careers best suited to you include but aren't limited to:

- Politician
- Lawyer
- Entrepreneur
- Financial advisor
- Sales director
- Pilot
- Performer

If you're an 8W9 (Eight with Wing-Nine), you're more cooperative, less intense, and more family-oriented, thanks to the influence of the Nine Wing. While the Enneagram Nine is pretty much the opposite of an Enneagram Eight, the effect of having this peace-loving conflict avoiding Wing soothes the aggressive nature of the Eight. The term "Bear" comes from that visual of having a powerful figure fully equipped with claws that will destroy you but snuggly in their own way and less prone to use their power unnecessarily. Of course, this may vary from person to person. Some people with this wing may be more influenced, so the peaceful quality may vary. As a general rule, 8W9 will be more open to other people's opinions, calm, reassuring, and tend to use less of an iron fist in their leadership style. The combination of aggression and indifference can be tricky at average and unhealthy levels. At unhealthy levels, the influence of this Nine

Wing leads to an unpredictable individual - calm and friendly one minute, then explosive and temperamental the next. For a healthy 8W9, the opposite is true, and in fact, we see this individual being extremely wise, generous, and protective of the people they love. They turn into great and benevolent patriarchs and matriarchs, at ease with themselves, strong-willed yet mild-mannered. People enjoy being led by such an individual.

As an 8w9, you probably want to be in a work environment where you have the space and freedom to be autonomous and still around others that you can help.

Careers best suited to you include but aren't limited to:

- Business owner
- Judge
- Activist
- Counselor
- Director
- Professor

The Arrows and what they mean

Your Enneagram personality type is linked to lines or arrows that show the path of growth or disintegration depending on where you are in life. When moving on a path of disintegration, a Type Eight will fall into the negative tappings of the arrow Five (5), where they suddenly become secretive and fearful. This is known as the Direction of Stress or Direction of Disintegration and typically occurs in the face of prolonged high stress. The other arrow indicates how a healthy version of your personality reacts and grows in more healthy environments. In this case, Type Eight integrates into the arrow Two (2), adopting the healthy aspects of the Two. That turns the lustful, controlling Eight into a more open-hearted, caring, and approachable individual. To understand the concept behind healthy and unhealthy levels, let's discuss the nine levels of development for a Type Eight.

THE 9 LEVELS OF DEVELOPMENT, FROM LOWEST TO HIGHEST

Levels of Development arise from Riso and Hudson's teachings and the founders of the Enneagram Institute, which is a great place to take your Enneagram Test. Their theory posits that all individuals fall into one of nine levels of functioning. The lowest level is nine, and the highest is level one. The levels are divided into a triad that subcategorizes these levels as healthy (1,2,3), average levels (4,5,6), and unhealthy levels (7,8,9).

Unhealthy Levels

Level 9: This is the lowest and most dangerous level for an adult Eight. Typically, we are all at this level during infancy. If we fail to rise to higher levels, we experience very unhealthy expressions and behavior with devastating consequences. For an Eight, this is where the person feels vengeful and murderous. They are barbaric with sociopathic tendencies. All this person cares about is getting what they want. When something or someone stands in their way, they may brutally destroy everything that doesn't conform to their will. Surrender is never an option.

Level 8: At this level, the Eight is delusional about their power, invincibility, and what they can achieve. They feel omnipotent and invulnerable and may recklessly over-extend themselves to get what they want.

Level 7: This unhealthy level for a Type Eight exhibits a hard-hearted, immoral, and potentially violent person. They hate any attempt to be controlled by anything or anyone and believe that might makes right. This Eight is completely ruthless and dictatorial in their approach.

Average Levels

Level 6: At this average level, we see an unhealthy Eight making progress toward maturity, but they are still combative, intimidating, aggressive, and use threats and reprisals to get obedience from others. Everything is a test of will for a Type Eight at this level of expression, and they're not very good at having healthy relationships because they use fear to control others.

Level 5: Type Eight is boastful, forceful, and ego-centric at this level. Being "the boss" and having everyone follow orders matters to this individual, and they want to impose their will and vision on everything. They don't see others as equal, so treating people with respect is challenging. What they want most is total domination of their environment.

Level 4: A Type Eight at this level of development is more enterprising, pragmatic, self-sufficient, and desires to have enough resources. They are risk takers who aren't afraid to bend the rules to get what they want. While they are hardworking and a little better with people, they struggle with emotions, often denying and neglecting their emotional needs.

Healthy Levels

Level 3: The individual at this level has grown into a healthy version of themselves, exhibiting more of their leadership and good people skills. This Eight is more decisive, authoritative, and commanding but in a more healthy way, championing people and protecting those under their wing. They are more honorable and courageously carry others with their strength.

Level 2: At this healthy level, we witness a mature individual who is self-assertive, confident, and strong, and people love to look up to this Eight. A Type Eight at this level has learned to stand up for what they need and want without stifling others, and they have respect for the people around them. They are extremely resourceful with a "can do" attitude that's contagious.

Level 1: Type Eight is at their best and healthiest version. Healing and transcendence bring about an individual who is self restrained and magnanimous, merciful and forbearing. They are courageous, passionate, driven, and willing to put themselves in serious jeopardy to achieve their vision. A lasting influence is what they care about. In many cases, these individuals achieve historical greatness and true heroism.

ENNEAGRAM EIGHT'S PASSION

The Eight's Passion or deadly sin is lust. It typically expresses itself as intensity and excessiveness. Eights tend to think that anything worth doing is worth overdoing.

What the Eight needs is innocence. This is the virtue that will bring much-needed openness and calmness. It will enable the Eight to be more vulnerable and to respond (rather than react) in a fresh way to each moment without judgment or force. If you're reading this and recognize that you're an Eight, this is the work you must do. Bring yourself back to wholeness by embracing your innocence.

CHILDHOOD AND EMOTIONAL PATTERNS FOR A TYPE EIGHT

The Eight's belief that vulnerability is a sign of weakness likely started in childhood. For most Eights, their childhood environment had plenty of turmoil, and conflict or combat was necessary to survive. Perhaps due to violence, neglect, or simply being the youngest or smallest in a big family, the Eight child saw the need to adopt a tough persona. They decided to grow up quickly and portray a "strong" personality because vulnerability or "softness" would lead to rejection, hurt, or betrayal. If they had a relatively nurturing childhood, they'd probably take on a strong protective role (especially when raised with a single mother). And if they came from an abusive childhood, they'll live in constant anticipation of rejection and betrayal. The more rejected they feel, the more they harden their hearts and become aggressive.

As adults, Eights carry the same worldview and do everything in their power to maintain an upper hand in all circumstances. They are the ones people turn to and rely on when in need of guidance and strength. While this does make them quite formidable, it also makes it hard to develop an intimate connection because they never want to let their guard down. The childhood would is experienced in behavior even as an adult through anger, avoidance of affection, imposing their control and will on others, etc.

To heal the childhood wound, an Eight must reconnect with their Higher Self and recognize that vulnerability is strength. They must learn to practice self-compassion and recognize that it's okay to trust and lower their guard with a small trusted group of people. As an Enneagram Eight, your path to healing begins the moment you become aware that you have a need to be seen as a strong unstoppable, impenetrable force at all times.

SUBTYPES FOR TYPE EIGHT

The Enneagram profiling system allows for 3 subtypes in each type. These are Self-Preservation, Social, and One-to-One (Sexual) variants. Remember, all three instinctual variants exist in all of us, but the order in which they stack up determines their influence on our lives. One will be most dominant and the easiest for you to resonate with and observe as behavior and thought patterns in your life. The second will feel a little neutral and less influential, and the third will be the least significant. The third instinct becomes a blind spot for many because it's underdeveloped and out of their conscious recognition. Depending on which instinct is most dominant, it will shape your unique personality and how you approach life as an Eight.

Self Preservation Eight (SP)

SP Eight possesses the quality of seeking satisfaction at all costs. SP Eights are strong, direct, aggressive, and highly productive. They are great at getting results and often the pillars of strength for many as they take on the role of guardian, father, or mother figure. They are protective of their family and loved ones and are most concerned with survival and meeting their needs. If their conditions aren't met satisfactorily, SP Eights forcefully push things forward without guilt until they get what they want.

Social Eight (SO)

The SO Eight is the most rebellious of the subtypes and enjoys being a rebel and trailblazer. They enjoy being the group leader because they are intense in their desire to create change and authentically stand out. SO Eights are pretty impulsive, and their key quality is possession. They are driven by the need to accumulate power and influence so they can serve a worthy cause.

One-to-One/Sexual Eight (SX)

The SX Eight is the countertype of the Eights, and their key quality is solidarity. It's easy to mistype this Eight for a Type Two because, unlike the SP Eights and the SO Eights, these individuals use their power and influence more in the service of others rather than asserting their own needs. They are extremely sensitive to injustice and unfair social norms. SX Eights are loyal and protective and believe it's their duty to protect and shield their people from harm, unjust authority, and other abusive powers. While they aren't big on emotions and vulnerability, they tend to be more open, receptive to feedback, and have close allies they trust.

CHAPTER 20
WORK AND LIFESTYLE TIPS FOR TYPE 8S

As part of your discovery and transformation, it's essential to recognize your triggers, the areas that you struggle with most, and where your opportunities for growth lie. Let's start with some of the struggles associated with your Enneagram Type.

STRUGGLES OF AN ENNEAGRAM EIGHT

Impatience

All Eights hate being around people who procrastinate or easily get distracted. They also can't stand waiting too long for results because they want results immediately. This quality of impatience can become a struggle if you don't find a better perspective when approaching big goals. Most of the time, it takes teamwork to achieve grand visions.

What to do: Be mindful of the goals and milestones you set for yourself and your team. Realize that people move at different paces, and some accomplishments do take time. Focus on progress instead of getting angry and impatient at the missing results.

Intimidating to others

Many people find you highly intimidating and perhaps too aggressive. That's probably because you hate sugarcoating things or beating around the bush. Some call it "intense," others call it "aggressive," and you don't get it. But it is something that's going to impact all your relationships.

What to do: Recognize that you are intense by nature and perhaps overly direct. With that awareness, approach your interactions mindfully and see if you can recognize instances where it's better to be calmer and let go a little. What would happen if you worked on bringing in a little more zen and harmony? Would you be less stressed? or healthier? Grateful?

Vulnerability and letting your guard down

Having a heart-to-heart and letting your guard down is tough. Ever since you can remember, you always needed to keep your defenses up to survive. Emotions and being vulnerable are signs of weakness, right? Turns out that's not entirely true. This struggle is real for all Eights until they learn how to rise to the higher levels of development and heal.

What to do: I know a part of you craves intimacy and tenderness. There is a way for you to be strong and still allow a few trusted people into your softer, gentler side. So let me encourage you to explore more about this topic.

Putting too much pressure on yourself

With big ambitious goals and the need to be the leader and protector of your universe, it's easy to put a lot of pressure on yourself. Asking for help is something all Enneagram Eights struggle with because it could lead to feelings of inadequacy or weakness. So I'm not suggesting you become a sissy, but I encourage you to delegate where needed. Having control of your life doesn't mean carrying the whole world on your shoulder. That need to constantly "run things" can become exhausting for yourself and others.

What to do: Invest a little time each day to have some quiet time where you can reflect, reset and regenerate. This quiet time will help you sort out your priorities and thoughts and help you feel more clear-headed and calm. Get in touch with nature by swimming in the ocean, hiking, biking, or walking in the local park.

ENNEAGRAM TYPE EIGHT UNDER STRESS

Enneagram Eights are typically stressed when they feel like they are being micro-managed, have to follow instead of lead, or can't see progress toward a goal. They also hate being around wishy-washy, lazy or manipulative people. As strong-willed as they are, feeling like they are not in control of things or dealing with failure can become highly stressful. But perhaps the thing that quickly causes a downward spiral to disintegration is a lack of challenge.

If you're an Eight and stress is mounting, don't wait for things to get out of hand. Instead, give yourself some distance from the thing stressing you and just allow yourself to decompress. Get clear-minded about the situation, and don't allow anger or feelings of injustice or rejection to crowd your thinking. Tune into your breathing and help your body calm down. If there's someone you trust, this would be a good time to let your guard down and share what's stressing you. Remember, letting someone in doesn't make you weak. It helps you gain perspective. And once you've got perspective and clarity, make your next move. You may not solve the entire issue instantly with a single move, but you should be fine as long as progress is made.

RELATIONSHIPS

Enneagram Eights are passionate, protective, daring, intense, purposeful, authentic, dynamic, and invested in their relationships.

In romantic relationships, Eights are interested in having a partner who can challenge them to become their best self. They seek loyal and independent partners who aren't afraid to go after what they want in life. To some, this might be too intense. In fact, some do perceive Eights as being overly competitive and a little intimidating. But if you're an Eight, then you also know there's a hidden softer layer that you only allow a chosen few to experience and those that do stick with you for a long time.

Relationship tips

Eights need to be the leader in the workplace, and they want to be responsible for the significant challenges and issues. They need a dynamic work environment with people who trust that their leader will get the results.

RELATIONSHIP TIPS WITH OTHER TYPES

Here are some ways to improve your relationships with other Enneagram Types.

Type 8 & Type 1: With a Type One, the relationship is based on truthfulness, fairness, and a lot of intentionalities. The One offers a systematic, detailed approach to life and your relationship. You and your partner are justice-oriented, responsible, and firm in your convictions. At the same time, you bring a sense of protection and deep loyalty that's comforting to your partner. Your relationship can be highly hospitable, family-oriented, and vibrant when operating at healthy levels. As a couple, you stay active, succeed in your careers, travel, and take any chance to change the world for the better.

A challenge that might create tension is how you prioritize your energies. You're more open and expressive of your anger. At the same time, the One is more self-controlled, carefully choosing their words and trying their best to repress anger. Your partner can easily get frustrated with your outbursts, and you might feel like you're being controlled. Grow together by reminding each other that you're on the same team.

Type 8 & Type 2: The relationship is passionate and energetic with a Type Two. You both see something needed in the other. You need that compassionate, gentle warmth that you want to protect, and your partner is drawn to your power and tenacity. The Two softens your edges, and you empower the Two to set healthy boundaries and learn to be more assertive. At healthy levels, you bring out the best in each other.

A challenge you might face is when you have a difference in opinion or a disagreement. You might also get into trouble for being too self-reliant and guarded, especially if still at average levels where opening up to intimacy is an issue. You might feel overwhelmed or smothered by the Two's need for constant affection. Meanwhile, your independent streaks could be interpreted as a loss of love by your partner, making them demanding. Grow together by continuing to develop to higher levels and embrace the safety and security you provide for one other.

Type 8 & Type 3: With a Three, you have a powerful dynamic relationship built on mutual respect, trust, and love. You are both intense, influential, and lively. That kind of passion and assertiveness enables you to go after anything you want in life. The relationship is highly satisfying because you finally find someone who can match your energy yet complements you in many ways. The Three finds a safe place to land because you aren't easily swayed and enjoy the high energy of your partner. They are

never intimidated by your power, which is very comforting. You can finally let go of control a little because you know your partner is competent and responsible.

When your personalities clash, you might experience a challenge, especially when you fall to average and unhealthy levels. Just as you positively match each other's energy, the same is true when things go dark. You easily see the Three's outer mask, which can create doubt about your partner's authenticity. Your fear of betrayal can create tension, and unfortunately, when the Three reads this tension, they tend to withdraw. Grow together by learning to let go, trust each other more, and add more fun to the relationship. Things don't always need to be controlled and zipped up.

Type 8 & Type 4: With a Four, your relationship is filled with passion and intensity. It's authentic and deep. The Four offers sensitivity and emotional vulnerability, and you bring practicality, strength, and protection to the relationship. There's a magnetic pull between you as you constantly seek to understand and conquer the mystery of one another.

A challenge you'll encounter is during the conflict. Explosive tempers and disagreements can quickly get out of hand, given how emotionally reactive you are. Neither you nor your partner like to be controlled, and you're both highly expressive, meaning it's easy to say things you might regret later. Because you're both reactive and enjoy the excitement, it's easy to get into cycles of fighting and make-up. While that might keep things interesting for a while, it's not healthy for a lasting relationship. Grow together by increasing the level of compassion you express, especially during conflicts. Work on rising to higher levels of development to become less reactive and remind each other that what you want is to be fully heard and understood.

Type 8 & Type 5: With a Five, the relationship is deep, loyal, and autonomous. You both share that independent streak and find something needed in the other. The Five often feels as misunderstood in the world as you do and that bonds you together in a strange way. The Five offers you deep, thought-provoking conversations and makes you aware of higher knowledge and the impact your actions have in life. You help the Five become more practical and in tune with their power and intuition.

A challenge in this relationship comes from the fact that you both seek to isolate in different ways. You desire to be entirely self-reliant through attaining physical and material resources. The Five takes pride in needing nothing and wanting less physical or material attachments. When this goes too far, it can drive a wedge between you, especially when you refuse to admit your needs to each other. Grow together by learning to acknowledge that you have needs. It's okay to have needs, whether physical, emotional, intellectual, or spiritual. Recognize that you both crave a more profound connection that can only come from intimacy and embracing vulnerability together. It's scary but worthwhile if you do it together.

Type 8 & Type 6: Everything is an open book with a Six. The Six craves safety and security. Your partner feels they can trust and depend on you through your protective, decisive, and transparent nature. You like the loyalty and dependability of the Six. You're both direct in communication and get everything out on the table.

A challenge you might face in this relationship is mistrust and reactivity during conflicts. Things go wrong when you don't feel like you can trust each other. The Six might find your bullish approach off-putting and destabilizing. You might see the constant questioning and concern as a lack of trust. At this point, you might walk away, especially if you suspect rejection. Grow together by reassuring one another that you're looking out for each other and that your relationship is safe. Avoid always attempting to control the situation. Instead, work on creating safety and keeping communication open.

Type 8 & Type 7: With a Seven, the relationship is full of fun, adventure, optimism, and boundless energy. The combination of both your energies is explosive in a positive way. The Seven helps you lighten up and have fun; you help the Seven become more practical, attentive, and grounded in the present moment. You're both assertive, dynamic, and captivating. There's never a dull moment in your relationship.

A challenge in this relationship comes from your values and how you approach conflict. You might see the Seven's cheerful disposition as lacking maturity and authenticity. And when someone isn't authentic, you have a hard time letting your guard down. The Seven might find you too controlling, leading to a battle for autonomy. Grow together by slowing down long enough to notice your reactions. Ask yourself if overreacting is helpful or healthy for your relationship. Be more present and mindful. Encourage each other to work through unpleasant and uncomfortable emotions.

Type 8 & Type 8: The relationship is mirrored with a fellow Type Eight. You're both strong-willed, intense, powerful, and protective, and you just get each other. You know you can fully trust each other, and you love the respect you have in your relationship.

You lead a dynamic lifestyle because you constantly challenge each other to grow and improve. There's never a dull season in your world.

A challenge that may arise here is how similar your temperaments are. Given your intensity and explosive nature, especially if anger hasn't been resolved, it's easy for things to get out of hand. If you feel like you're being controlled by the other, you may shut down and withdraw from the relationship. Grow together by maintaining an open dialogue. Work on rising to higher levels of development together and embrace vulnerability. Genuinely affirm one another. Do it frequently.

Type 8 & Type 9: With a Nine, the relationship is stable, calm, nurturing, and autonomous. The Nine helps you learn when to pull back and how to relax. They make you feel loved and accepted just as you are. It's safe to be yourself, and the relationship is earnest and respectful. You help the Nine find their voice, see their value and assert themselves more. You both enjoy the connection, companionship, and safety you offer one another.

A common challenge here is how you both deal with anger and conflict. Although you're both in the body triad, you deal with anger by expressing it, while a Nine deals with it by avoiding it at all costs. So when conflicts arise, a Nine will withdraw, become distant, and disengaged. That's probably going to frustrate you tremendously, and in your heated temper, the Nine becomes resentful of your behavior. They will never stand their ground and fight no matter how offended they feel, and it's easy for you to misread that. Grow together by allowing each other space to process negative emotions. Be open about this and communicate how you'll deal with disagreements. Create enough time to do some fun activities together regularly to keep that connection strong.

AFFIRMATIONS:

- I am in control of my own destiny.
- Life happens for me, not to me.
- I value collaboration over competition.
- I am learning to let my guard down and trust those I love.
- I aspire to lead and inspire others.
- What I judge in others is what I judge in myself.
- I am kind to myself and others.

Remember affirmations only work when what you say deeply resonates with how you feel. Make sure you pick affirmations that align with your emotions for best results.

DAILY TIPS FOR GROWTH AND HAPPINESS

Schedule reflective time

It's essential to have a little downtime where you can just "be." Allowing yourself time to clear your mind and refocus will give you more energy and open you to higher perspectives. It will also keep you calm. Speaking of calm, let's talk about some mindfulness practices.

Practice mindfulness daily

Find some mindfulness practices that can enable you to process emotions, stay calm, and ground yourself at any given moment. Some can become part of your morning or evening routine, while others can be little hacks to deploy whenever necessary. Consider journaling, meditation, yoga, nature walks, mindfulness baths/showers, and deep breathing. Find what works best for you. These mindfulness practices will keep you calm and in the present moment. The more present you are, the more powerful you become.

Embrace vulnerability and your softer side

This will be scary at first. You don't need to become vulnerable with everyone. Study some materials to learn more about what it means to be vulnerable, tune into your emotions, and pick a few people you can choose to let in. Brené Brown is an expert on vulnerability, so you might want to Google her and watch one of her many videos that describe what vulnerability is and its benefits. The most important thing is to shift that core belief around vulnerability so you can realize that it makes you stronger, not weaker. Take your time working on this, and trust that even a little bit of vulnerability will positively affect your relationships.

CHAPTER 21

ENNEAGRAM TYPE 9

THE PEACEMAKER OR MEDIATOR

The last two chapters of this book are dedicated to uncovering the details of the Enneagram Type Nine, commonly referred to as the peacemaker or mediator. As you may have guessed, this personality type values keeping peace above all else. Internal and external peace should be maintained at all costs, even if it means avoidance or conformity. Nines are absolutely loveable, and everyone loves to be around them because they are always accepting, assuring, loving, easygoing, and just nice to be around. They are very stable in their behavior and often too willing to just go with the flow even when it doesn't serve their highest good. Nines are part of the body triad along with Eights and Nines, which means they rely primarily on their gut to navigate life. Their core unresolved emotion is Anger, but unlike the Eights, who have no difficulty expressing their temper, the Nines do everything possible to suppress it. They don't redirect it inwardly as the Ones do but instead try to pretend it doesn't exist. There might be a leak often, and you may notice bouts of temper, which can be shocking for others around them since they come across as cool and calm. They are a brewing ocean of stored anger and resentment.

Nines always strive to achieve harmony and peace. Their primary focus is comfort. Driven to connect with the people around them and be part of a group or community, Nines have a tendency to go the extra mile to be part of the group, even if it means disregarding their own needs or feelings. So it's not uncommon for a Nine to feel like they've lost their identity or don't have a voice in a relationship or group, especially if the people involved are stronger in opinion and personality. When operating at high levels of development and at their best, Nines are optimistic, creative, all-embracing, and excellent at bringing people together and healing conflicts. Nines become stubborn, lethargic, and indecisive at average and unhealthy levels.

STRENGTHS OF A NINE

The Nine can see multiple people's perspectives at once. That's a unique quality that no one Enneagram Type possesses. It makes them great peacekeepers and mediators.

Another strength they possess is actively listening without judgment, offering a sense of acceptance and love. When you confide in a Nine, you feel "heard and seen," which makes people love being around them.

Key personality traits of a Nine

- Calm, collected demeanor
- Mellow and soothing
- Likeable
- Wide circle of acquaintances

Common hobbies for a Type Nine

- Meditating
- Exploring nature
- Napping
- Relaxing with friends
- Practicing spirituality

FEARS AND WEAKNESSES

Type Nines have a basic fear of loss and separation. They can't stand being separated from others and really fear a loss of any kind, unresolved conflict, and relational tension. Nines are known to avoid anything and everything that could jeopardize their sense of harmony because they never want to feel fragmented. Deep down, all a Nine really wants is to feel at peace all the time.

Another issue for Nines is the fear of being too needy and thus pushing people away. That's why Nines always strive to be the glue of a group or relationship. They do everything to maintain a harmonious state, even if it overrides their desires. Often this fear comes from the belief that their opinions and needs don't matter as much as those of others. This tends to become a weakness for Nines because as they avoid all disturbances and confrontations, they may become resentful. Average and unhealthy Nines also develop passive aggressive tendencies.

Somewhere along with their upbringing, they picked up the message that their opinions, needs, wants, and dreams don't matter. So you'll often find Nines struggling to express their own ideas or even saying "no" to something.

What's the Basic Fear driving this behavior? The fear of losing their connection and becoming fragmented.

How does this basic fear often manifest itself?

Of all Enneagram Types, Nines are the most self-forgetting. It's the most pronounced expression of their fear. They'll forget their thoughts, priorities in life, and goals. When faced with a conflict or confrontation, the Nine's natural reaction is to disengage from people and their emotions even when it would be in their best interest to participate.

Another expression of this fear is the brewing inner resentment and the outer passive aggressive behavior that's quite common for average and unhealthy Nines. At times their need to avoid anything that disrupts harmony can cause them to become numb to situations and negative emotions, leading to withdrawal.

DESIRES AND MOTIVATIONS

The basic desire for a Type Nine is to have inner stability, peace of mind, and to feel whole and connected. They are motivated to keep peace around them, which causes them to be very agreeable. Unfortunately, leaning too much into this motivation does lead to unhealthy behavior that creates inner turmoil for the Nine. That's why it's crucial for a Nine to be intentional and courageous enough to decide what kind of peace and harmony they want in life, and then practice speaking up when their peace is violated instead of withdrawing.

Nines desire to feel safe, accepted, and heard even though they may not articulate it. This desire feeds into the way they exist in the world, how they see themselves, and their relationships with others. Feeling seen, heard, and accepted energizes a Nine and further deepens their connection with others.

Core values

- Harmony
- Gentleness
- Compassion
- Balance

Type Nine celebrities and famous people you might know to include Former President Barack Obama, Former President Ronald Reagan, Former President Bill Clinton, Actor Morgan Freeman, Actress Audrey Hepburn, Actress Whoopie Goldberg, Former President Abraham Lincoln, Her Majesty Queen Elizabeth II, Actor Clint Eastwood, and the 14th Dalai Lama.

Wondering if you're a Type 9? Here are some personality indicators

1. Conflict of any kind is the worst thing in the world.
2. Coffee is the magic miracle working drink you can't live without.
3. It's easy for you to see all perspectives at any given time. One of your greatest strengths is that you can hold and understand multiple perspectives.
4. You struggle to believe that you matter and that your presence matters.
5. Routines rock, and you can't figure out how other people live without routines.
6. You easily procrastinate, especially when overwhelming kicks in.
7. Comfort matters to you a lot.
8. You're naturally very stubborn when you want to be.
9. Getting started on a new project is hard for you, but you see things through once you get started.

10. You're very easygoing and always going with the flow.
11. The outdoors is very calming and peaceful for you. You absolutely love the great outdoors.

YOUR WINGS

Wings are the numbers adjacent to your Enneagram Type. As a Nine, you have -

- The Enneagram Nine with an Eight Wing: "The Referee"
- The Enneagram Nine with One Wing: "The Dreamer"

While you may have tendencies that lean into both wings at various stages of your life, you'll likely be more dominant in one than the other. This will be your most influential and Dominant Wing.

Meaning of your Wing

If you're a 9w8 (Nine with Eight-Wing), you're more energetic and confident. The combination of being a personality that tries to avoid conflict at all costs yet is influenced by a wing that absolutely loves conflict is quite complex. It turns out, however, that this combination works in your favor because the Eight Wing gives you more access to your anger, so you're no longer afraid to express that emotion. However, because you're fundamentally a Nine, you never let it get out of hand, and you quickly restore peace once you've made your point. At unhealthy levels, the influence of this Wing can lead to a lot of contradicting behavior. You might be highly energetic in one area of your life while being neglectful and lazy in other parts. You can also become too stubborn, depressed, and resistant to any help, only to lash out in unexpected bursts of violence. However, when operating at healthy levels, the influence of the Eight Wing makes you assertive, strong, and still gracious. You're still gentle and easygoing, but you can slam down hard when the situation calls for it.

Common career types that best suit a 9w8 include:

- Judge
- Social worker
- Religious worker
- Veterinarian
- Salesperson
- Diplomat
- Editor

If you're a 9w1 (Nine with One-Wing), you're more idealistic and disciplined. The combination of a Nine and One (depending on how strong it is) can turn into a very principled, focused, and often more confident individual. The influence of the One-Wing gives you a stronger sense of right and wrong and a more idealistic view of the world. Your patient openness combined with the objectivity of a One makes you a wonderfully non-judgmental counselor with outstanding levels of integrity. On more unhealthy levels, the conflict avoidance typical of a Nine can mix with the smoldering resentment of a One to produce a particularly sarcastic and indirect form of anger. When things get pretty bad, this unhealthy Nine can feel morally superior towards others, and perfectionism can take over in certain parts of their life while they become totally neglectful in other areas.

But of course, there are also the healthier versions of a 9w1, and that's when you become really organized, rational in your thinking, and highly productive. You become more effective and willing to share your ideas with others. Your active listening skills and ability to see things from multiple perspectives are enhanced by the influence of the One Wing, making you a powerful counselor or mediator.

Common career types that best suit a 9w1 include:

- Museum curator
- Counselor
- Nurse
- Diplomat
- Environmental scientist
- Human Resources Director
- Pharmacist

Arrows and what they mean

Your Enneagram personality type is linked to two other "lines" or points that are worth noting. These lines are called arrows, and each indicates how you show up at your best and worst. One Arrow called the Arrow of Disintegration shows the lines of stress (your path of destruction), and for you, that path lies in number 6. As you disintegrate, you pick up the unhealthy habits of an Enneagram Six and become more anxious and worried. We'll talk more about stress and how to avoid falling into disintegration in the next chapter.

The other line connected to your Enneagram type is 3, which is the Arrow of integration. That means that moving on the path of growth and integration, you take on healthy traits from a Three that make you self-developing, productive and energetic like healthy Threes. To understand the relationship between these arrows and how we fall into unhealthy patterns or rise into healthy ones, let's discuss the nine levels of development. The goal here is to identify where you might be and move toward the highest level, i.e., healthy level 1.

THE 9 LEVELS OF DEVELOPMENT, FROM LOWEST TO HIGHEST

Levels of Development arise from Riso and Hudson's teachings and the founders of the Enneagram Institute, which is a great place to take your Enneagram Test. Their theory posits that all individuals fall into one of nine levels of functioning. The lowest level is nine, and the highest is level one. The levels are divided into a triad that subcategorizes these levels as healthy (1, 2, 3), average levels (4, 5, 6), and unhealthy levels (7, 8, 9).

Unhealthy

Level 9: This is the lowest and most destructive level for an adult Nine. We're all usually at this level during infancy, so there's nothing wrong with this level. Problems arise if we fail to grow, develop, and spiritually mature because then we get stuck expressing behaviors associated with this level, which leads to terrible consequences. For a Nine, this is where they become completely self abandoning, severely disoriented, and catatonic. Some even struggle with multiple personalities, feeling like shattered, empty shells.

Level 8: A this level, a Type Nine is numb, depersonalized, and unable to function as a productive member of society. In an attempt to block out anything that could affect them, they become completely disconnected from themselves and the world.

Level 7: The Nine at this level feel incapable of facing problems. Everything is simply too overwhelming making them highly repressed, undeveloped, and ineffectual. Some are so neglectful to the point of being a danger to others.

Average

Level 6: At this level, the Nine have grown enough to the point where they aren't completely disconnected and numb. However, they are still pretty bad at dealing with disturbances and conflict. Stubbornness is a key quality at this stage of their growth, and they tend to minimize problems. Some are fatalistic and resigned as if nothing could be done to change things, while others become frustrated and angry by their tendency to procrastinate and engage in conflict-avoidance.

Level 5: At this level, the Nine is active but inattentive and disengaged. They walk away from problems and prefer to sweep things under the rug to avoid discomfort. This Nine is emotionally indolent and totally indifferent to anything that threatens the harmony they crave.

Level 4: This Nine is the classic easygoing "yes" man or woman who will do anything to avoid conflict and maintain connections with others. They are highly neglectful of their own needs and tend to fall into conventional roles and expectations, losing their identity to accommodate others. This type of Nine often deflects and can be known to be quite philosophical as a coping mechanism to appease others.

Healthy

Level 3: At this level, the Nine have grown into the mature healthier levels of development. Here we witness an individual who is optimistic, supportive, reassuring, and great at communication. That facilitates connection and oneness in all their relations. They have a healing and calming influence that brings people together and facilitates great mediation.

Level 2: At this level, the Nine is emotionally stable, serene, self-accepting, and more in tune with their identity. They are at ease with life, themselves, and others. Their expression and behavior are simple and innocent. Everyone loves Nines at this level of development because they are genuinely nice, unpretentious, good-natured, and trusting of themselves and others.

Level 1: This is a Nine at their best and highest expression. The individual is autonomous, fulfilled, content, and intensely alive at this level. They have great equanimity and are fully present to themselves, making them even more powerful and present in their relationships. This Nine has found oneness with self and a deep connection to others simultaneously.

ENNEAGRAM NINE'S PASSION

Type Nine's Passion or deadly sin is sloth. It typically expresses itself as indifference. Nines like to spend energy keeping the outside world out and the inside world in instead of paying attention to the self. They seem to have psycho-spiritual laziness, which unfortunately causes them to lose touch with their core self.

What the Nine needs is the right action. This is the virtue that will bring much-needed aliveness, engagement, commitment, and a willingness to act on what they know is right. If you're reading this and recognize that you're a Nine, this is the work you must do. Bring yourself back into wholeness and reconnect with your core self. Come back into the present moment, right action.

CHILDHOOD AND EMOTIONAL PATTERNS FOR ENNEAGRAM NINE

One might wonder, how did the Nine develop this belief that their presence doesn't matter? Most of the time, it begins in childhood. As a child, a Nine might have been deeply connected to the parental figures but in some way felt overlooked. The Nine might have learned that it's easier to keep the peace by not being assertive at some point. They may have been a middle or younger child unable to get the attention they needed or a quiet voice whose opinion got lost in a sea of loud or forceful voices. Regardless of the details, the Nine got used to blending in and just going along to avoid getting upset or creating disturbances. Most Nines are easygoing children who accommodate the family's needs, cause no trouble, never ask for anything, and are great at keeping peace when conflicts arise.

Because Nines are so connected to the people they love, they have difficulty differentiating their own feelings from others. Connecting to their parents gives them a sense of identity. And so, they grow up out of tune with their own feelings and always in the background of other people's stories.

As adults, the same patterns show up as Nines assume it's best to reserve their involvement and numb themselves to pain. Because nothing is important to them, nothing can let them down. This is a perspective held by many wounded Nines. Their childhood wounds show up as procrastination, indecisiveness, sleeping for long periods, and indifference.

To heal the childhood wound, a Nine must reconnect with their Higher Self and realize that their ideas, opinions, and presence matter. They need to cultivate a new mindset concerning their value and worth. As a Nine, you need to remind yourself that you have a unique identity to you alone and that your true identity is whole, always peaceful, and confident.

SUBTYPES FOR TYPE NINE

The Enneagram profiling system allows for 3 subtypes in each type. These are Self-Preservation, Social, and One-to-One (Sexual) variants. Remember, all three instinctual variants exist in all of us, but the order in which they stack up determines their influence on our lives. One will be most dominant and the easiest for you to resonate with and observe as behavior and thought patterns in your life. The second will feel a little neutral and less influential, and the third will be the least significant. The third instinct becomes a blind spot for many because it's totally underdeveloped and out of their conscious recognition. Depending on which instinct is most dominant, it will shape your unique personality and how you approach life as a Nine.

Self Preservation Nine (SP)

SP Nines are most concerned with meeting their physical needs. They enjoy keeping a routine around their activities and creating comfort in their lives. Peace and time alone are vital to them, and they often become irritable and stubborn when others upset their balance. SP Nines prefer to collect things to fill that void to avoid dealing with their internal states.

Social Nine (SO)

SO Nines work hard to support their groups to find belonging and comfort. Their essential quality is participation because they like to feel like they are part of something. As the countertype of the subtype Nine, these individuals work really hard to keep the people in their life happy. Sometimes, that leads to overworking, pain, or stress, which they tend to hide by putting on a happy front to avoid burdening others.

One-to-One/Sexual Nine (SX)

SX Nines have the quality of fusion because they are most likely to merge with a significant other as a strategy to feed their sense of self and guarantee comfort. SX Nines tend to feel most secure when partnered with others and may find it challenging to be on their own. Boundaries? What boundaries? For an SX Nine, aligning their personal desires and attitudes with the other is what matters, even if it means sacrificing their Truth and personal identity.

CHAPTER 22

WORK AND LIFESTYLE TIPS FOR TYPE 9S

As part of your discovery and transformation, it's essential to recognize your triggers, the areas that you struggle with most, and where your opportunities for growth lie.

STRUGGLES OF AN ENNEAGRAM NINE

Burying your voice under politeness

Placating others is detrimental to your happiness, yet many Nines are guilty of this. They say "It's fine" or "you decide" just because they want to avoid conflict. Unfortunately, opting to be polite and speaking up, especially when someone offends you, only leads to buried resentment, loneliness, and pent-up anger. It makes you feel invisible, unheard, and unloved even when the person didn't mean it to happen.

What to do: Talk about your interests with others and invite people to do things with you that you love. Refuse to say "whatever you want" for a week and notice how much better you'll feel.

People who love you will not be offended when you have an opinion. They'll respect and love you even more for your presence.

Putting things off until the last minute

Procrastination is real for Nines. Putting things off until the last minute just seems to be second nature, but unfortunately, it's neither healthy nor productive.

What to do: Make a short list of what you want to accomplish each day. Break down large goals or projects into mini milestones and then set some deadlines for the mini goals. As you complete each mini goal, reward yourself with a small treat. When the big project or goal is achieved, do something wonderful to celebrate yourself.

Indecisiveness

This is a struggle all Nines experience. The gift of seeing and holding multiple perspectives when interacting with others also means that you may have difficulty choosing a side or having a clear opinion. You're not alone. Most Nines say it's tough to know what they really want or believe, especially when presented with equally good options. Average to unhealthy Nines struggle even more with this because, in addition, they are also out of tune with their own desires.

What to do: Stop trying to make everyone happy. It's impossible to lead a life where you make everyone happy all the time. In the end, you forget your own Truth. When you feel undecided or unsure about what you want, say, " I need some time to think it over." Practice a little assertiveness and watch the magic it will add to your relationships.

Denying your anger

All Nines desire inner and outer peace. They want to be authentic and understood. Being the calm, nurturing one is of great importance to them, and unfortunately, that tends to create conflict avoidance. It can also lead to denial because rather than acknowledge this emotion or the offense they've taken, they'll try to suppress it.

What to do: Become more aware of that anger and resentment brewing inside since childhood when you learned that your presence doesn't matter. Being cool on the outside but irritated on the inside doesn't do you any good. It certainly doesn't bring you closer to the lasting wholeness you seek. So it's time to let it go. Notice how often and quickly you get judgmental, irritable, or tense. What underlying issues are at play when you feel these emotions? Try to voice them sooner rather than later to avoid having outbursts that you'll regret.

ENNEAGRAM TYPE NINE UNDER STRESS

Enneagram Nines typically get stressed when dealing with peer pressure, when they are forced into a position they're not comfortable with or when there's conflict around them. They hate being with people who enjoy drama or divas who enjoy having the spotlight. It's also super stressful for a Nine to have too many demands on their time. But perhaps the most dangerous habit for a Nine is to suppress their anger for too long.

If you're a Nine, you already know you get stressed when you say "yes " to things you don't really want to do. You also know that relationships are essential to you, so you must find a way to be yourself and still maintain those healthy relationships. It comes down to developing enough courage to be yourself. Give yourself permission to own your voice and use it in your relationships. Start by finding healthy ways to "let out" all the anger, frustration, and resentment you've suppressed. Process this anger either on your own through journaling and mindfulness practices or with the help of a professional. Learn to tune into your body and emotions. What are your physical, emotional, and spiritual needs? What do you love? Recognize that you are a unique individual with unique strengths, talents, and dreams. Be courageous enough to pursue the things you love and allow others to support you on this journey. Trust that your loved ones will continue to love you even when you say no to their requests.

RELATIONSHIPS

Nines are supportive, patient, encouraging, pleasant to be with, and accepting in all their relationships. Because they value harmony and comfort, all their relationships are easygoing and offer soothing comfort and stability. Nines long to be loved and cared for in a way that supports their peace and creates genuine, deep, connected love.

Nines can merge so strongly with their partner that they lose their individuality and personal identity in romantic relationships. They are usually willing to go above and beyond to create a loving space for the relationship to thrive.

Creating an environment that fosters goodwill and togetherness is important to Nines. They are very good at keeping peace within a team setting. They are steady and balanced in their approach to projects and relationships at work. However, their main challenge is to stay focused on priorities and speak up when they need to stand their ground, especially when it's uncomfortable, or a potential conflict ensues.

RELATIONSHIP TIPS WITH OTHER TYPES

Here are some ways to improve your relationships as an Enneagram Nine.

Type 9 & Type 1: With a One, you're in a stable, comforting relationship. With a Type One also being part of the body triad, you both give of yourselves physically to others, often with minimal attention to yourselves. You take great satisfaction in loving others in the community and giving generously to each other. The One brings a sense of duty and is more task-oriented, which is very helpful to you because it enables you to create routines that facilitate the peace you desire. Your kind accepting nature is attractive to the Type One and causes them to be more self-forgiving and self-accepting. You also remind Type One to choose people over principle, and they help you speak your Truth more. You both value being ethical and considerate. It's a very purposeful and enriching relationship.

A challenge you might encounter here, especially if you're both operating at average or lower levels of development, is your unresolved anger. Both you and Type One tend to deal with anger in unhealthy ways. You're concerned with repressing anger to keep peace and avoid conflict. At the same time, Type One is concerned with suppressing it appropriately. That pent-up anger can leak out as explosive tempers or resentment/stubbornness/silence, all of which are unhealthy for a lasting relationship. Grow together by finding healthy ways to deal with anger and other negative emotions. Work on rising to higher levels of development as a couple and affirm one another and the relationship during tense situations.

Type 9 & Type 2: With a Two, you're in a warm, nurturing, loving, serene and comfortable relationship. It's a highly engaging and reciprocal relationship. You're not demanding and always accepting, which allows the Two freedom to tend to their own needs. You also offer the Two a sense of security and stability where they feel loved for who they really are. Your partner helps you get in tune with your own desires and offers a warm embrace for you to express them.

You might encounter a challenge if the Two's helpful energy feels overwhelming for you. Perhaps you find them too emotional, which might create an inner disturbance. Twos are also quite action-oriented while you're easier going and like to move through life in a relaxed way. When you become upset, you tend to become passive and distant, while Twos become resentful and indignant. To work through all these issues, grow together by learning to acknowledge and resolve conflict as it comes up. Take the time you need to process, but don't repress negative emotions. Remind each other that true peace is cultivated when conflict is addressed in healthy ways.

Type 9 & Type 3: With a Three, you're in a dynamic, purposeful, encouraging, and driven relationship. You give your partner the space to be themselves with total acceptance and love. The Three offers you encouragement to find your voice and follow your dreams. They see potential in you and become your biggest cheer-leader. There's great balance and reciprocity in this relationship, and you enjoy the peace, respect, and trust that you both provide.

A challenge you might experience, especially when you're both at average or lower levels of development, is during the conflict. The Three might feel like you're holding them back from achieving their goals, and you might feel like they're just neglecting you and making no time for the relationship. Your easygoing nature can become a frustration for the Three, who see it as inaction. You might feel pushed and rushed to keep moving faster and chasing after targets. Instead of withdrawing, grow together by remembering that there's good in both of you. The speed you both operate is neither wrong nor right, so you just need to find a balance that works. Keep an open dialogue and encourage each other to grow to higher levels.

Type 9 & Type 4: With a Four, the relationship is deep, sensitive, empathetic, and non-judgmental. You both value independence and want to have a deep connection. The Four offers that acute emotional awareness that encourages you to go deeper and voice your emotional experiences. Your non-judgmental nature enables the Four to move toward self-love instead of drowning in self-doubt. As the pragmatic one in the relationship, you help keep things stable, which keeps the Four grounded. You also become a lot more energetic and outgoing under the influence of the Four.

A challenge you might face here comes from your opposing reactions to stress. When you get stressed or, a conflict arises, your natural response is to disengage to maintain peace. Meanwhile, the Four is emotionally reactive under stress and conflict. So when you withdraw, your partner sees that as a lack of presence and an unwillingness to work through things because they believe that it's important to express all feelings. While that becomes an overwhelming and unsettling experience for you, grow together by learning to give each other the chance to process stress in a manner that suits your personality. Consider finding healthy stress-releasing activities that you can use, e.g., journaling. When you do discuss the issue, do so with compassion and thoughtfulness.

Type 9 & Type 5: With a Five, you're in a thoughtful, calm, stable, accepting, and autonomous relationship. Because both of you can easily get overwhelmed by the demands of the world, you establish structures that enable you to maintain the peace you want. As the Five puts their attention on you with great curiosity, you're able to put to words your thoughts and ideas. That creates more self-awareness and a sense of connection. You help the Five feel more relaxed and at ease which is significant because often, Fives feel like they can't be comfortable in this world.

A challenge you might face in this relationship is, of course, when things get challenging. Your easygoing nature can turn passive-aggressive and quite stubborn during the conflict. On the other hand, Fives are rational and objective, so they'll have difficulty understanding your reaction. The other thing is that you both prefer to take time alone to process thoughts and feelings before verbalizing them, which can cause conflict to simmer for days before being fully addressed. Sometimes, you may cope with conflict in your own separate ways and never really come together to discuss and resolve it as a couple. Grow together by finding ways to stay grounded and present, especially when things get tough. Consider sitting down together to write down your feelings and discuss them until the issue is resolved.

Type 9 & Type 6: With a Six, you're in a stable, comforting, predictable, loving relationship. The Six offers loyalty, security, unity, affection, quick-mindedness, and action, which enables you to be a more active force in your life. Your calm demeanor stabilizes the Six, who tends to be more skeptical and alert to issues. Healthy interdependence is assured in a relationship like this, and you both enjoy it.

A challenge you might face with this relationship is again during moments of stress. The Six's questioning can feel accusatory to you, while your withdrawal can feel like abandonment to your partner. Another issue is that Sixes tend to be reactive during the conflict, primarily if operating at lower levels of development which, as you know, is very uncomfortable for your personality. Grow together by keeping an open dialogue and supporting each other in voicing your needs and wants. Be clear about what you really want in life and how you want your relationship to be.

Type 9 & Type 7: With a Seven, the relationship is full of energy, adventure, and optimism. The Seven brings fun, assertiveness, and self-confidence and helps you break out of your shell and try new things. You bring steadiness, calmness, and a personal touch that the Seven finds attractive. Both of you like looking to the bright side of life, and your differences complement each other.

A challenge you might face is the stubbornness you both have. When it rears its ugly head, things can go wrong, especially if you don't take the time to work through the issues as they come up. The Seven is more likely to surface conflict since they don't want to be trapped in unpleasantness. Unfortunately, this need to quickly move past negative issues can often leave you feeling trampled or overlooked because they don't give you enough time to fully process the issue. Another issue is that because you like to avoid conflict, sometimes your partner may not be aware that something is going wrong until it's almost too late. That can be very hurtful for the Seven. Negative issues and uncomfortable emotions are challenging for both of you, so after the tough talk, reward yourselves with something fun. Affirm each other regularly. Grow together by learning to work through conflict sooner rather than later.

Type 9 & Type 8: With an Eight, the relationship is dynamic, earnest, and autonomous. The Eight offers protection, and you admire how tenacious and powerful they are. You help the Eight learn how to relax, let their guard down and embrace their softer side, and they help you see your value and become more assertive. Given your strong values of fairness, justice, respect, and trust, the relationship feels safe. You enjoy the companionship and connection you share.

A challenge you might face in this relationship is rooted in the fact that you both belong to the body triad, yet you handle anger quite differently. When things get difficult, you tend to withdraw and become passive-aggressive and disengaged, which angers the Eight, who would prefer to confront the issue head-on. The Eight pushes harder when things get tough, and they want you to stand your ground and fight it out. This kind of intensity can feel overwhelming to you. Grow together by keeping an open dialogue and finding a middle ground when dealing with conflict. I also encourage you to plan something fun together and regularly affirm each other.

Type 9 & Type 9: With a Nine, you're in a mirrored relationship. This is harmonious, deeply serene, and comforting. The companionship is beautiful, and you offer each other constant acceptance and encouragement. Since you both like predictability, you've set a routine that works for you and built a safe, comforting space for each other. You're patient with one another and like to draw each other out without being too intrusive. While you make time to have fun and be silly, what you love most is the connection you've built and the life you have together, taking life's challenges in stride.

A challenge you may encounter, especially if operating at average or lower levels of development, is the struggle with knowing your identity, unique desires, and opinions. It takes a while for you to process things, and because you like to stay positive, conflict can be a scary thing. When things aren't going well, you both withdraw and disengage. Grow together by choosing not to ignore each other's withdrawing behavior. Instead of entertaining passive aggressive behavior, take the initiative. Remember that true peace often requires good communication. A little healthy conflict and addressing unpleasant emotions together are recommended. Just approach it with compassion and be patient with each other as you learn to work through conflict.

AFFIRMATIONS

- My feelings are valid and important
- I give and receive love generously
- I am not responsible for other people's happiness
- I am willing to express my Truth and desires
- Obstacles are opportunities for growth

Remember affirmations only work when what you say and feel are in synch. Choose only the affirmations that resonate deeply with you.

DAILY TIPS FOR GROWTH AND HAPPINESS

Practice being more assertive when interacting with others.

This will require practice and may feel very uncomfortable at first, so start with small action steps. For example, stand in front of a mirror and say something you've always wanted to say to someone in your life. Practice standing in a confident, assertive posture. Notice your body language and tone as you speak. Once you get comfortable with the mirror, test it on your mom, sibling, or someone you trust. Grow into being more assertive gradually.

Process your anger and negative emotions

Promise yourself to continually work through any and all negative emotions. This will help you get better at handling conflict without being confrontational. You can use journaling, talking it out with a friend, or any other healthy form of expression you prefer.

Be more active in life and explore new things

I know you like to stick to routines and stay in your comfort zone, but it will do you a world of good to add a little planned adventure every so often. Try going on hikes alone, go for dips in the lake or nearest sea. None of these activities are likely to lead to human conflict. If you like fishing, then do that often. Find something adventurous you enjoy doing alone.

Daily exercise

Put in some daily workout to move your body and break a sweat. It will give you an energy boost and enable your brain to avoid falling into procrastination. Do you enjoy jogging in the neighborhood? Weight lifting in the gym? Swimming? It doesn't matter what you do. Just do something you want and enjoy regularly.

CONCLUSION

We've taken a deep dive into all the Enneagram Types, their basic fears, and desires. You've learned about subtypes, struggles for your Enneagram type, childhood wound and emotional patterns that show up as an adult, and relationship tips. Now that you understand more about your Enneagram Type, it's time to draw parallels and manifest positive changes in your own life.

As you've learned, there is no Enneagram type that's better or worse than the other. We all have strengths and weaknesses, positive and negative traits that need improvement. At different phases in life, we might be operating at unhealthy, average, or healthy levels, and it's up to us to keep rising higher.

If you have successfully identified your Enneagram Type, you can use the suggestions given to improve your life. It begins by becoming self-aware. Go back to the chapters that cover your type and decipher the intricacies you may have missed to better understand yourself. Get to know your motivations, weaknesses, core values, and how you tend to react under stress. Read through the different levels of development and see if you can identify where you're currently placed so you can further work on cultivating habits that will lead you to your best self.

This book might be over, but your journey is just getting started. Awareness and commitment to this journey of self-discovery are mandatory if you wish to experience transformation. Take this knowledge and implement it. Find small changes you can make so you can see the benefits of the Enneagram firsthand. Remember, all the books in the world cannot bring you the healing, wholeness, and success you deserve. For that to happen, your participation and continuous integration are required. The Enneagram system will change your life if you work it. Take this next step and keep learning, implementing, and growing.

I wish you all the best.

RESOURCES

Traditional Enneagram (History). (n.d.). The Enneagram Institute. Retrieved May 20, 2022, from https://www.enneagraminstitute. com/the-traditional-enneagram

The Enneagram Personality Test. (n.d.). Truity. Retrieved May 22, 2022, from https://www.truity.com/test/enneagram-personality-test

User, G. (2021, May 13). *Enneagram: Arrows*. Cloverleaf. Retrieved May 20, 2022, from https://cloverleaf.me/blog/enneagram-arrows

Cloete, D. (n.d.). *Wings, Arrow Lines, Integration and Self-Mastery*. Integrative9. Retrieved May 20, 2022, from https://www.integra tive9.com/enneagram/wings-lines-integration/

A. (2021, January 14). *Arrows: Each Type at their Best & Worst*. Full & Free Enneagram Co. Retrieved May 20, 2022, from https://kris tirowles.com/best-worst/

Learn More About All 9 Enneagram Types | Your Enneagram Coach. (n.d.). Enneagram Coach. Retrieved May 20, 2022, from https://www.yourenneagramcoach.com/types

The Nine Enneagram Types. (n.d.). THE ENNEAGRAM AT WORK. Retrieved May 20, 2022, from https://theenneagramatwork.com/nine-enneagram-types

www.ingramcontent.com/pod-product-compliance
Lightning Source LLC
Chambersburg PA
CBHW022045020426
42335CB00012B/547